Biotechnology

A Guide To Scientific Approach And
Technological Innovation

*(A Comprehensive Book On The Biotech
Patent Laws Includes Biotechnology
Business)*

Stephen Siler

Published By **Phil Dawson**

Stephen Siler

All Rights Reserved

Biotechnology: A Guide To Scientific Approach And Technological Innovation *(A Comprehensive Book On The Biotech Patent Laws Includes Biotechnology Business)*

ISBN 978-1-77485-510-2

Legal & Disclaimer

costs, and expenses, including any legal fees potentially resulting from the application of any of the information provided by this guide. This disclaimer applies to any damages or injury caused by the use and application, whether directly or indirectly, of any advice or information presented, whether for breach of contract, tort, negligence, personal injury, criminal intent, or under any other cause of action.

You agree to accept all risks of using the information presented inside this book. You need to consult a professional medical practitioner in order to ensure you are both able and healthy enough to participate in this program.

Table of Contents

Table of Contents

Introduction

Biotechnology is the use of biological agents or mechanisms for the production of useful products and executing processes to serve various needs. The biological agents used in this context include microorganisms, plants animals and cells components, and macromolecules that are biological (proteins and enzymes, which are typically). Biotechnology generally is a process of receptions that allow the production of valuable products using industrial methods using the vital biological processes in living organisms.

In the middle of the 20th century, innovative methods of biotechnology were developed in the wake of the fact that improvements of microbiology techniques and chemical mutagenesis allowed to develop extremely productive strains. Many beneficial microbiological substances were discovered for individuals as well as, more importantly different chemical compounds for drugs.

Since the 1980's. Genomic sequencing research started to be conducted around the mid-1990s. A project involving the human and animal genomes was created. This led to the development of biotechnological innovation development, as well as other advancements in the genome of microorganisms. It was a new phase in the growth of biotechnology, a modern biotechnology that was primarily focused on medicine. More then 70% studies and research results are linked to the manufacture of biomedical and pharmaceutical substances.

Biotechnology is often used in food and medicine as well as to resolve problems in the fields of environmental protection, energy as well as in research. [3]

In medicine, biotechnological strategies and methods play an important part in the development of biologically active compounds and medications to aid in the early detection and treatment of various ailments. Antibiotics comprise the most extensive class of pharmaceutical substances that are prepared by microbiological synthesis. is accomplished using microbiological synthesizing. Generative engineering of Escherichia yeast, coli as well as cultured mammalian and insect cells that are used for the production of insulin, a growth hormone as well as human interferon a variety of antiviral and antibacterial vaccines have been developed. Modifying the nucleotide sequences in the genes that code for the respective proteins, improve the structure of hormones, enzymes and antigens (the known as"protein engineering"). The most significant discovery was the creation of Keller in the year 1975. Milshtein employs a hybridoma method to make monoclonal antibody of that desired specificity. Monoclinal antibodies serve as reagents that are unique to the treatment and diagnosis of various ailments.

The aim of this study is to examine the major direction and application of the latest biotechnological techniques in the manufacture of pharmaceuticals.

Chapter 1: Introduction Biotechnology

1.1. Biotechnology

The field of science that studies biological systems, such as living organisms or components of them that are able to create or manipulate products to meet specific goals, such as genetically modified food as well as drugs animal products, enzymes plants.

1.2. The history of Biotechnology

Biotechnology is in line with the latest methods for enabling recombinant DNA technology, also known by the name of genetic engineering. The story of biotechnology began with the study of zymotechnology (study in yeast ferment) which began with the study of brewing techniques. However, following World War I, zymotechnology increased to address significant industrial problems. And the ability of industrial fermentation brought about biotechnology. The oldest biotechnological methods can be found in the process of the process of microbial maturation. The beginning of the Babylonian tablet in 6000 BC was first discovered in 1881. It was described in the process of brewing beer.

Around 4000 B.C. Unleavened bread was made using yeast. The Sumerians could consume about twenty kinds of beer during the third millennium B.C. The 14th century was the time when the first vinegar industry was developed in France close to Orleans. In

4

1680 Antony Van Leeuwenhoek first saw yeast cells using his new microscope as well as Louis Pasteur highlighted the proliferation of lactic acid caused by bacteria in 1857. In the late nineteenth century, a huge number of scientists and industrialists were involved in biotechnology and a major biosanitary program was developed throughout Germany as well as France. From 1914 until the year 1916 Delbruck, Hennerberg, and Heyduck discovered the widespread usage for yeast within the industry of food. In the at the same time, Acetone Butanol and glycerin were identified in bacterial cultures. The year 1920 was when Alexander Fleming discovered penicillin and the production of penicillin started in 1944.

Table 1.1. The development of biotechnology over time. Biotechnology

The first appearance of biotechnology occurred more than a century old. Biotechnology advances have led into the struggle against SARS-CoV-2 disease (2013) and COVID-19, the COVID-19 outbreak. First bionic vision developed in the US provides hope to blind people all over the globe in 2010. A group of researchers from J. The Craig Venter Institute made the first synthetic cell in 1998. A draft map of human genome, which contains over 30,000 genetic codes was compiled in 1997. Scientists are trying to introduce Earth in Dolly sheep, which is the first mammal in the mammal family. Transgenics were first created in 1969. The enzyme was produced from in vitro cells for the very first time in the history of science around the year 1953. Biologists James Watson and Francis Crick identified the double helix in DNA back in the year 1943. Canadian researcher Oswald Theodore Avery discovered that DNA is an important genetic carrier in 1928. Scottish Bacteriologist Alexander Fleming discovered the use of penicillin, an antibiotic, in 1919.

1.3. Biomanufacturing

Biomanufacturing is a type of manufacturing process that makes use of biochemical systems (e.g. microorganisms, plants, resting cells, tissues, animals enzymes, synthesized in vitro (enzymatic) methods) to produce important commercial biomolecules with value added for the food, agricultural materials, energy, or pharmaceutical industry. These products could be isolated from other natural sources, like blood, microbes' cultures and animal cells or plant cells. They were developed in specific equipment or specially-designed cultivation conditions. The enzymes and cells utilized could be naturally occurring or altered by metabolic engineering, genetic technology, synthetic biology and the engineering of proteins. Biomanufacturing, though it has played a crucial part in the last three industrial revolutions, the process of biomanufacturing 4.0 is expected to be one of the key foundations of the sustainable revolution that is taking place in the 21st century.

The three industrial revolutions of the past are

i. 1. The initial industrial (technology) revolution started with Great Britain in the late 18th century. There were a number of instances of mechanization in the textile industry driven by coal mining and steam engines

ii. II. The industrial revolution began in the first decade of the twentieth century of the USA and featured instances of the widespread utilization in internal combustion engines fuels that were liquid (fossil) fuels and electrification. Mass production was using moving assembly lines

iii. 3. The 3rd industrial revolution featuring examples of extensive use of computers as well as the internet. Today, manufacturing is becoming digital, a process known as industry 4.0

1.3.1. Biomanufacturing and manufacturing history

The biomanufacturing history is divided into four revolutions, similar to industrial revolutions. New directions for Biomanufacturing 4.0 could revolutionize biomanufacturing in order to create various products from foods, renewable energy as well as medicines and drugs and also materials that are superior to the existing biomanufacturing methods in terms of yield volumestric productivity, titer biomanufacturing costs and sustainability.

Unintentionally attempt to segment the history of biomanufacturing according to the types of products biocatalysts, biocatalysts, as well as tools (Fig. 6.1.) in which new technologies and products are typically developed in the same time and in synergy to lead to the biomanufacturing revolution. Typically, the need as well as items (or money) constitute the main driving factor, while technology helps to commercialize products and meet market demand provide a model for technology development.

	Pre-modern BM	BM 1.0	BM 2.0	BM 3.0	BM 4.0
Need & Products	Fermented products	Primary metabolites	Second metabolites	Proteins Enzymes	Renewable energy, New food, Better life
Methods	Mixed cultures + solid state ferment.	Mono-culture + anaerobic liquid ferment.	Mono-culture + aerobic liquid ferment.	rDNA tech + cell cultures	?? IPS + ME&SB + PE + ivSB
Key persons & time	Louis Pasteur 1860s	Chaim Weizmann 1910s	Alexander Fleming 1940s	Paul Berg 1980s	

Figure 1.1.The development of bio-manufacturing's history

1.4. Branchings of Biotechnology

There are various areas of biotechnology, like

1. Industrial biotechnology

2. Medical biotechnology

3. Biotechnology of animals

4. Plant biotechnology

5. Environmental biotechnology

6. Biotechnology in the aquatic environment

1.4.1. Industrial biotechnology

It is concerned on the industrial production of beneficial organic compounds through microorganisms, notably fungi and bacteria like acetic acid citric acid, acetone Glycerine, glycerine, etc. as well as antibiotics such as streptomycin mitomycin, penicillin and others.

1.4.2. Medical biotechnology

It is concerned with the diagnosis of various illnesses as well as the production on a large scale of hormones and medications, including interferon and insulin in humans and vaccines for chickenpox the poliovirus, rabies, etc. and growth hormones like bovine. In the field of medical research genetic engineering has assisted in the mass production of blood serum hormones, proteins antibiotics, as well as other essential medical products.

1.4.3. Biotechnology for animals

It concerns the creation of transgenic animals that can increase production of milk or meat, with the ability to resist various diseases. This also covers in-vitro fertilization as well as transfers of embryos to animals, such as man.

1.4.4. Plant biotechnology

Plant biotechnology is the combination of engineering genetics and cell cultivation. It is concerned with the growth of transgenic plants that includes the growth of haploids. resistance to stressors both biotic and abiotic the rescue of embryos, multiplication of clonal clones cryopreservation and more.

1.4.5. Environmental biotechnology

It focuses on cleaning industrial effluents and wastes and treatment of wastewater and controlling plant insects and diseases with the help of biological agents like bacteria, viruses, fungi and others.

1.4.6. Biotechnology in the aquatic environment

It focuses on marine life in order to improve the supply of food in the world increase the safety of seafood as well as quality, and to discover novel compounds that benefit the health of humans and medical treatments. It is also utilized for exploring new ways to treat and monitor diseases as well as bio-processing and restoration and protection of and preserving the ecosystem of marine life.

1.4.7. Red biotechnology

Based on the Biotechnology Innovation Organization (BIO) it is a health-related field which is responsible for creation over 250 different vaccines, antimicrobials, regenerative techniques and prosthetics.

1.4.8. Biotechnology raw

It is used in more than 13 million farms across the globe to combat pests and to plant crops, and also to protect the crops against microbes and extreme weather conditions, like frost and drought.

1.4.9. White biotechnology

The industry is working to improve the efficiency of production processes, to develop biofuels, as well as other techniques to improve the efficiency of the industry and sustainable.

1.4.10. Yellow biotechnology

This department is focused on food production includes, for example, studying ways to lower the amount of saturated fats in cooking oils.

1.4.11. Blue biotechnology

The use of maritime resources is to search for cosmetics, marine and health-related products. Additionally, it is an area that is utilized to obtain biofuels from microalgae.

1.4.12. Gray biotechnology

Its aim is to protect and restore the pollution-ridden environment by, as stated in the previous paragraph, bio-remediation procedures.

1.4.13. Golden biotechnology

Also called bioinformatics, it is the process of acquiring the storage, analysis and classifying information from biological sources specifically those that pertain to DNA sequences and amino acids.

1.5. The applications of biotechnology

Biotechnological innovations are already aspect of our life, and we can find it in the supermarkets and pharmacies and in many other locations. Furthermore, in the last few years biotechnology has emerged as one of the weapons used in the battle against the COVID-19 global epidemic because it aids in defining the viral genome and comprehend the way our immune system combats viruses.

Biotechnology will play an important part in the future of society by preventing and containing possible viruses, however it is not the only one of the many applications. The advancement of growth hormone, insulin and cell identification as well as genetic therapies and vaccines like Hepatitis B are just a few of the most important elements of biotechnology and its interaction to genetic engineering. The development of new biotechnology and handicrafts just started. In the near future, we may be able to make concrete plant species that alter color as they encounter explosives, clothing and footwear made from a synthetic web spider, etc.

In addition to foods that are genetically modified as well as biotechnology-based products like WEMA has created a insecticide and plant that is drought-tolerant that could be considered to be essential to fight food in Africa. Through bioremediation that are extremely beneficial in the regeneration of the environment, the properties of microorganisms' structures such as fungi, enzymes and plants are utilized to clean up the environment.

1.5.1. In Food Manufacturing, Fermentation

The fermentation process is possibly the oldest biotechnological breakthrough. In the past, more than 10,000 years humanity was producing vinegar, wine, beer and bread with microorganisms and yeast, specifically. Yogurt was produced using the lactic acid bacteria that were found in milk and the mold was then used to produce cheese. These methods are still utilized to make modern food products. But, the food cultures that are employed are refined to preserve the most desirable traits and best quality of the food products.

1.5.2. Food Storage

Drying or salting food to stop spoilage from bacteria is performed before anyone is able to comprehend the reason for it or understand what causes the food to go bad at all in the first instance.

1.5.3. Industrial Fermentation

The discovery that the enzymes of yeast in 1897 converted sugar to alcohol, led to the development of industrial processes like Butanol as well as acetone and Glycerol. Fermentation is still used in a variety of biotech firms, typically for the production of enzymes for processes for pharmaceuticals, ecosystems as well as other industrial processes.

1.5.4. Separation (Quarantine)

Segregation as a method to stop the spread of disease took place long before the genesis for the illness was discovered. But, it demonstrates that there was a prior acceptance that the disease is transmitted from an infected individual to an uninfected person who may develop signs of the illness.

1.5.5. Optional Reproduction

Enhancing yields by choosing varieties from productive or healthier plants to create an improved crop that has the best traits is an approach to earlier harvesting technology. Farmers are realizing that selecting seeds from the most productive crops will eventually increase the demand of the following crop. In the mid-1800s, Mendel's study of genetics of peas enhanced our understanding of the nature of inheritance and created breeding patterns (now known as hybridization).

15 years ago, significant advancements were made by genetic engineers and biologists which we are hoping to address many of the urgent problems, particularly the food and energy crises in order to deal with the increasing population of the world. Ore deposits are becoming increasingly costly and difficult to extract out of the Earth's crust. Microorganisms are able to enhance the extraction of minerals from low-grade ore and also in homes that contain excessive

quantities of heavy metals or other toxic substances. When these technologies are employed in an industrial setting they can make an eco-system.

Table 1.2.Principal Bio-Industry products

Chapter 2: Microorganisms In Biotechnology

2.1. Microorganisms in Biotechnology

2.1.1. Fungi/yeast

They are microorganisms that can be which are found in soils as well as on plants and are of great commercial significance in the industry of fermentation. They are used in industrial settings to produce high-value products like steroids and a broad variety of antibiotics. Apart from being used for the production of chemical compounds like amino acids as well as glycerol they are also employed for the production of bread, beer and bio-ethanol.

2.1.2. Aspergillusniger

Aspergillusniger which is a black mould is not one organism. It comprises a variety of strains with different biochemical and morphological traits. This group is typically utilized in fermentation to aid in the manufacturing of enzymes, organic acids and antibiotics. It is typically located in moist areas. Aspergillusniger is usually used in the manufacturing of citric acid. It is typically the preferred organism because it is simple to handle, is able to ferment various substrates, and is able to produce large yields.

2.1.3. Saccharomyces cerevisiae

Saccharomyces cerevisiae, which is the budding yeast, is usually found as a diploid i.e. it contains two complete sets of genomes, one for each parent. Similar to Escherichia Coli, it is completely sequenced genome. It is unicellular and is found in soils and the exudates of fruit. It is used in baking wine, brewing, and baking. Saccharomyces cerevisiae cannot utilize pentose sugars for its sole source of energy. It is used for industrial production of ethanol. Despite being known to be resistant to temperatures that are extremely high (above 35 degrees Celsius) species that can ferment between 40 between 40 and 45 degrees Celsius has been recently chosen for use in the process of advancing cultures and selecting survivors following the heat shock process. In the ethanol fermentation process, S. cerevisiae has been found to be more resistant to inhibition than the majority of species of bacterial.

2.1.4. Bacteria

Bacteria are ubiquitous and can be present everywhere. Their industrial applications include bioremediation, bioenergy production in addition to chemical manufacturing. They have been utilized in bioremediation, particularly for cleaning up of waste in wastewater treatment facilities and are also used to generate energy in the form methane, H2 and methane, and. Additionally they are also used to produce essential chemical compounds like organic acids Butanol as well as 1,3 propanediol.

Pseudomonas like Pseudomonas Aeruginosa are used for bioremediation of harmful chromium in electroplating effluents.

Bacillus species (Bacillus subtilis) are used for the commercial production of chemicals, such as Vitamin B2 (riboflavin).

Clostridium makes use of a variety of celluloses and sugars as carbon sources. It transforms these substances to alcohols i.e. alcohol, organic acids and ethanol, i.e. the acetic acid. The members of this genus include the industrially significant Clostridium acetobutylicum. This is mostly used in the production of acetone, ethanol and Butanol.

On the other hand bacteria that produce lactic acid (LAB) create the lactic acid using simple sugars. They include Lactobacillus species which are used extensively for the production of fermented foods like yogurt.

Bacteria that produce lactic acid are commonly employed in vegetable fermentation including beets as well as carrots.

Table 2.1.Commercial application of bacteria

2.1.5. Zymomonasmobilis

Zymononasmobilis is a Gram-negative, facultatively anaerobic bacterium that is known for its ability to make various substances like levan, oligosaccharides (ethanol), ethanol and the sorbitol. The importance of ethanol production is increasing due to a variety of reasons. It is highly efficient in the production of ethanol due to its capacity for the high rate of glucose absorption. It is also able to endure high levels of ethanol of up to 16 percent per litre. Additionally it is believed to be tolerant of excessive sodium levels. Its nutritional requirements are easily found in industrial waste. Additionally it's able to degrade raw sugar, sugarcane juice and sugarcane syrup into alcohol.

Z. mobilis generates ethanol through the Entner-Dodoroff pathways that is activated under anaerobic conditions. This pathway creates 1 mole ATP in each mole of glucose. This means that when compared with Saccharomyces cerevisiae Zymomonasmobilis requires more energy in the process of producing ethanol. However research has shown the fact that Zymomonasmobilis creates 5 times as much alcohol than other microorganisms that produce ethanol such as the brewer's yeast Saccharomyces cerevisiae.

2.1.6. Clostridium

Clostridium bacteria have a rod-shaped shape and are Anaerobic Gram positive bacteria. They produce spores and are mostly isolated from potatoes soil water, air and dust. They are known for their production of H2, ethanol, as well as other solvents like Butanol and Acetate. As a result, they are named Acetone-butanol-ethanol (ABE) producing clostridia. ABE producing clostridia goes through two stages. The first phase is connected with the production of acetate and butyrate and the second is distinguished by the production of solvents, acetone Butanol as well as Ethanol. Solvents are created due to acid accumulation in the first phase, which is then favored by the production of solvents.

Clostridium Acetobutylicum and Clostridium beijerinckii are both widely used to aid in ABE production and have been observed to thrive on a variety of substrates. The 21 substrates can be any of the domestic waste, agricultural wastes or industrial waste. Clostridia that use cellulosic biomass as their primary carbon source, like Clostridium thermocellum, typically employ a variety of cellulitic enzymes. These enzymes reside on the cellulosomes, which are located on the cell's surface. They break down cellulose into glucose that is then transformed into useful substances. Clostridia has also been utilized in a variety of studies to boost H2 production. It produced as high as 27.2 milliliters of H2 per each 10 g/l glucose by using C. Acetobutylicum in unsaturated flow-reactor. Clostridium Acetobutylicum is also found to produce lactate and the acid acetic.

2.1.7. Escherichia Coli

Escherichia coli is a rod-shaped Gram-Negative bacterium which belongs to the family of Enterobacteriaceae. It is an anaerobe facultative that has been the most extensively studied and is an entire genome sequence. As compared to other microorganisms E. coli is advantageous due to its capacity to produce all major sugars and produce an ethanol-based mixture along with organic acids. The reason for this is its genetic structure.

2.2. Role of Microorganisms and Biotechnology

Microorganisms that are part of the fermentation process are the most important source of energy which converts substrates into valuable products. The effectiveness of these microorganisms is due to their genetic composition. They have special enzymes that are capable of making substrates more metabolized. They breakdown a range of substrates into various compounds, and produce a variety of gas and heat. Today, fungi and bacteria are used extensively in industries to make useful chemicals and gases, like ethanol, methane, acetic acid and H2. Bacteria are mainly used due to their ability for genetic engineering as well as their high rate of growth.

Chapter 3: Maromolecules In Biotechnology

3.1. Introduction to Macromolecules

Macromolecules consist of monomeric components with a basic structure. Macromolecules are living, solid cells composed of four kinds of carbohydrates, proteins nucleic acids, and lipids. However, inorganic salts as well as minerals make up a smaller part of the cell weight.

Living organisms consist from a few kinds of atoms, including carbon nitrogen, oxygen, sulfur, phosphorus, and ions like sodium and magnesium, chloride as well as calcium, potassium, and trace elements like cobalt, iron manganese zinc, copper, etc. and macromolecules. The role that the carbon atom plays living systems is determined by its capacity to form strong bonds for the joining of other elements. Sometimes, they form rings and chains that form the cells of living molecules, which in turn is life itself. In these carbon structures different atomic groups are referred to as active groups (e.g. and hydroxyl carbonyl or carboxyl disulfide, methyl, ethyl amino group, ether and many more.) These groups provide particular chemical structures for the molecule. The molecules comprise diverse types of molecules which constitute living structures.

A variety of duplicate monomeric units from simple organic molecules are combined to make macromolecules. They constitute the primary elements of cells. They include polysaccharides, proteins, lipids, as well as nucleic acids . They are among the most widely-known macromolecules. Carbohydrates function as the most efficient source of bioenergy and lipids function as stored energy. Proteins are essential to processing the body's requirements and nucleic acids function as information molecules connected to genetic engineering and expression of this information. Tools for analysis are now the foundation of vast research in modern biology and industry of pharmaceuticals and chemicals.

3.2. Protein

Proteins are plentiful throughout the biosphere and are present in many different ways, each one suited to fulfilling specific biological functions. The first person to identify the entire amino acid chain of the insulin protein is Fred Sanger in 1953. Also they are made by amino acid. Natural proteins consist of 20 amino acids that are common. The most common amino acids include at least one code which will be found in DNA. Certain amino acids that are rare are also found in proteins that don't have DNA coded, however they are made up of different amino acids.

Plants can mix essential amino acids to create simple substances, however animals are unable to mix other essential amino acids known as essential amino acids. And these are required to be added to their diets to meet the need. Based on these amino acid are divided into three categories:

* Amino acids that are conditional (e.g. the amino acids arginine glutamine, cysteine ornithine, glycine and tyrosine proline, serine, and arginine)

• Non-essential (e.g. Alanine asparagine, arginine cysteine, aspartic acid, glutamine, glutamic acid serine, proline, glycine and the tyrosine)

* Vital (e.g. histidine, isoleucine, leucine methionine and phenylalanine tryptophan, threonine, and valine)

3.2.1. Structure of protein molecules

Proteins are made of amino acids and are bound through a peptide bond. The protein is gradually able to go beyond the normal binding and create a different type of bond, such as the effect of ionic bonds disulfide bond, hydrogen bonds, and hydrophobic bonds. These bonds play an essential part within the main, secondary, and higher protein structures. The amino acids that bind make up the peptide bond by an amide connection. The a-carboxyl atom of one amino acid reacts amino group alpha of another amino acid in order to create a bond through the dissolution of the water molecule in the peptide. Simple peptides comprise three, two or four residues of amino acids, referred to as di tri, tetra, and tripeptides and tetrapeptides, respectively. The peptide contains free carboxyl and amino groups, in which other amino acids can be synthesized into polypeptides. The protein may contain a variety of polypeptide chains.

3.2.2. The role of protein molecules

Proteins are created to fulfill diverse roles throughout biological organisms. In this way, they can be classified into the following seven categories.

I. Catalytic proteins or enzymes (lactase pepsin amylase, salivary kallikrein and the lingual lipase)

ii. Transport protein (hemoglobin, cytochromes and myoglobin)

iii. Storage protein (egg, ovalbumin, ferritin, and casein)

iv. Motile and contractile proteins (actin as well as myosin)

V. Structural proteins (collagen alpha keratin and elastin)

vi. Antibodies or immune proteins (immunoglobin, blood clots, venom, and the bacterial toxin)

vii. Hormonal Protein (insulin, oxytocin, as well as somatotropin)

Globular proteins are soluble in water and most are higher education-based that is composed of proteins e.g. protein to store and protect. Fiber proteins are not soluble within water, and possess secondary properties in the natural world, e.g., elastin alpha keratin. Three kinds of proteins are available in relation to their melting. Of these, synthetic proteins are made up of one chemical component along with amino acids. The amino acid component that is not present in synthesized proteins are known as "the synthetic" group. Combination proteins are classified based on the chemical characteristics that they belong to their group. For instance, lipoprotein is a source of some lipids in their implant (e.g. beta lipoproteins in blood) and similarly, glycoprotein (e.g. immunoglobulin) has carbohydrates and as does phosphoprotein. (milk casein) includes a class of phosphate. Metalloprotein also is a source of metals, such as iron (e.g. ferritin, for instance) and zinc (e.g. alcohol dehydrogenase) as well as copper (e.g. and Plastocyanin) and so on. as a synthetic compounds. Proteins are found in a variety of kinds of structures, including low and high, and residential structures. In the primary structures of amino acids proteins are placed in a sequential fashion within the polypeptide chain. A secondary arrangement is stable amino acids that create repeated patterns in the structure, or are created by local arrangements of atoms within a the polypeptide backbone. This does not contain the production of chain extensions.

3.3. Nucleic acid

Nucleic acids are biopolymers that have high molecular mass and mononucleotides as replicating elements. These structures form long polynucleotides, which are the genetic components of all living things.

There are two nucleic acid kinds: Deoxy Ribose Nucleic Acids (DNA) and Ribose Nucleic Acids (RNA). Through hydrolysis they release phosphoric acids as well as a pentose sugar as well as nitrogenous bases. The sugars in both DNA andRNA occur in furanose form . They are part of the beta 5-carbon sugar. It is commonly referred to as pentose sugar.

In DNA the oxygen atom is liberated by the carbon atom. The sugars are formed into esters and H_3PO_4 and form an array of 31-51 phosphodiester bonds in sugars that are close by. The nitrogenous base comes in four kinds of which two are originated from Purine and two are made from the pyrimidine. Purine bases are Guanine (G) and Adenine (A). They comprise the six-pyramid ring, which is paired with the imidazole rings of five members. The two pyrimidines include Thymine (T) and the cytosine (C) inside DNA and the uracil (U) is found in RNA in place of Thymine. Phosphoric acid creates an acidic environment for nucleic acids. The grouping of phosphate and sugar is involved in the creation and synthesis of nucleic acids. The nitrogenous foundations are linked to pentose sugar through beta glycosidic linking without the phosphate group to form nucleosides.

Nucleosides continue to break down in phosphoric acid, resulting in nucleotides, or in another words, nucleotide phosphoric isers nucleosides. These nucleotides do not constitute all that are needed to build a structure.

3.4. Lipids

Lipids are insoluble aqueous entities created by the condensation reaction between alcohol and fatty acids. They share a common formula R-COOH, where R stands for hydrogen, or groups such as C2H5, -CH3. The majority of natural fatty acids comprise Between 14-22 carbon atoms. Acids with high levels of carbon atoms tend to be less liquid. The hydrogen and carbon atoms create an naturally occurring hydrophobic or water-loving hydrocarbon. The longer the series of hydrocarbons grows, the temperature at which heating and melting for fatty acids is raised. When fatty acids are made up of two or more double bonds and are referred to as insatiable. Acids that have smaller than ten molecules carbon aren't in liquid form at room temperatures and sugar-free acids have lower melting temperatures than saturated acids.

Based on the number of carbon atomsin a molecule, the fatty acids may be classified into fatty acids that have an even chain (2 4, 6 for example, acetic acid or butyric acid) or odd chain fatty acid (that have an inequal chain of 3, 5 7 e.g. propionic acid or valvic acid). Based on the length of the chain of hydrocarbons, they can be separated into short-chains (with between 2 and six carbon atoms) and medium-chain (with 8-14 atoms) and a longer chain (16 to atoms) consisting of the 24 different fatty acids. The lipids and fatty acids play multiple vital biological roles within living creatures. They provide energy. They are located in cells' membranes. They are involved within the multi-cell responses and signature pathways, the cell-level transport systems, as well as bio-recognition sites. Lipids function as signals by way of hormones and cofactors, as well as pigments.

3.5. Carbohydrates

Carbohydrates are substances that make one of these substances in hydrolysis. They contain oxygen and hydrogen in the ratio of

2:1. In plants, they can be present in starch as well as in animals, they are known as glycogen. Carbohydrates can be broken down in sugars as well as non-sugars. Sugar is crystallineand liquid and has an appealing taste. The excess sugar is split into oligosaccharides, monosaccharides, and monosacc. When the chain is open one carbon atom is double-bonded to an oxygen atom, forming an carbonyl group. Monosaccharides are aldoses when the carbonyl group is found at the very end of the carbon chain. When the carbonyl group is in another position, the monosaccharide is a ketose--non-amorphous sugar, tasteless and insoluble in water. Extra sugar is divided into homopolysaccharides and heteropolysaccharides.

Table 3.1. It is the presence of sugars listed above and non-Biomed sugars

Chapter 4: The Fermentation Process

4.1. Fermentation

The word "fermentation" is an Latin verb that is derived from the word 'fervor and boil. The process of fermentation can have different significance to biochemists as well as industrial microbiologists. The biochemical significance of the process is related to the generation of energy by metabolic breakdown of organic molecules while its use for industrial microbiology is likely be more broad.

The term "fermentation" was used by microbiologists to define any process that results in the production of a product by the mass cultivation of microorganisms.

A product may be:

1. The cell itself: refers to the production of biomass.

2. The foreign product of a microorganism called the product of the recombinant DNA technology or a genetically engineered strains, i.e., recombinant strain.

3. Microorganisms' own metabolite: refers to the product that comes from an original or genetically enhanced strain.

4.1.1. The products produced by microbial activity

A variety of products are created by microbial activity through fermenting. Some of the most popular products are:

4.2. Different types of processes for fermentation

There are two main types of fermentation processes.

Submersion fermentation

Solid-state fermentation

4.2.1. Submersion fermentation (SmF)

Submersion fermentation takes place in fed-batch, batch as well as continuous. In the surface technique, microbes are grown in the surfaces of a liquid or solid substrate. Submersion processes are where microorganisms are grown inside the fluid medium. the medium is kept in the fermenter, and stirred until there is uniform distribution of the medium and cells. The majority of processes are aerobic, in which case the medium needs to be thoroughly aerated. The majority of industrial processes, i.e., production of proteins, biomass as well as antibiotics, enzymes and sewage treatment, take place through submersion processes.

4.2.2. SSF, or solid-state fermentation (SSF)

SSF is a solid state fermentation (SSF) is thought of as an important bioconversion method to change natural resources into a vast range of chemical as well in biochemical products. The process involves the fermentation of a substrate with microorganisms in the absence of flowing water. SSF is being utilized successfully for the production of food as well as fuels, animal feeds, and fuels as well as to degrade dyes.

A SSF is a process of fermentation that involves the use of solid substrates utilized with a tiny volume of water. SSF is a reference to natural environments of microorganisms , but puts them in the area of the substrates in order to attain more efficient growth of microbial life. Because SSF processes generally take place with low water activity One of the benefits is the lower demand for sterility which provides another opportunity for non-sterile fermentation. It is widely used within the industry of food for production of flavors, enzymes as well as organic acids.

They are commonly used to create hydrolytic enzymes, such as cellulases, xylanases and pectinases under nonsterile SSF conditions. It was confirmed that this SSF procedure and xylanase activity that resulted was identical in both the non-sterile and sterile conditions however, the latter condition can effectively reduce the expense of the procedure. With the development of improved reactor designs and the rapid advancement in bioengineering technology, SSF is becoming attractive for specific biotechnological uses.

4.3. The ranges of fermentation processes

There are five categories under which commercially significant fermentations can be classified as:

4.3.1. Processes involve the creation of enzymes by microbes.

Animals, microbes, or plants form the primary sources for commercial production of enzymes. Since enzymes are created on a massive scale through fermentation processes they possess a vast potential for economic growth. The introduction of recombinant technology DNA has allowed for the creation of animal-based enzymes from microbes. Through the development of DNA technology for recombinant synthesis it is now possible to make enzymes that are of interest from prokaryotes. Through the addition of activators and inducers to the media for production it is possible to increase your production process of these enzymes.

Table 4.1.Application of Enzymes

4.3.2. The process involves the production of metabolic compounds by microbes

The growth of the microbial culture is divided into four phases

1. Lag phase

After the inoculation process of cells into the nutrient medium the bacterial growth doesn't take place. The cells expand in size and mass, synthesising the population, but the number of cells remains unaffected for a while. There is a very high metabolic rate during this stage. This is known as the stage of adaption. There are many variables that affect this stage of growth, including the size of inoculum and the amount of time required for the synthesizing of basic coenzymes, as well as other variables.

2. Log phase

This is the period of exponential growth. In this stage the rate of growth of the organisms gradually increases. Cells grow at maximum proportion--conditions of incubation and constitution of the medium control the growth of cells.

3. Stationary phase

In this phase of growth the growth ceases for cells. Numerous factors play a role including an accumulation of inhibitory metabolites as well as a depletion of nutrients that are available. At this point the number of dividing cells is equivalent to how many dying cells. In this stage bacteria produce secondary metabolites.

4. Death phase

This phase is inverted of the phase log. Cell count decreases in this stage. The essential metabolites that aid in the development of cells, such as amino acids, protein nucleotides and lipids are created extensively during this stage. Metabolites produced in this stage are referred to as primary metabolisms. Many metabolites produced in this phase are of economic value. Wild-type organisms seek to synthesize the principal metabolite that is required to develop the organism. The production of large-scale quantities of the primary metabolites is attained by providing the right conditions that permit wild-type species to develop.

Table 4.2.Few significant commercially-priced products of metabolism

Table 4.3.Production of metabolites via diverse pathways that originate in Fungi

Table 4.4.Production of metabolites via microbes

4.3.3. The process involves the creation of microbial cells as products

Production of Bakers yeast on a massive scale was first established in the early 1900s. Through the 70s a tiny amount of continuous, large-scale processes to produce animal feed were identified. They were based on hydrocarbon sources which could not compete with the protein-rich feeds for animals and result in their extinction (the latter part of the 1980s)

i. the production of bakers" yeast

Protein consumed as a human food is composed of a smaller amount of microbial proteins than yeast. Human food is mainly comprised of edible macrofungi with some bread. Skimming was the initial method to industrially produce yeast strains from Saccharomyces cerevisiae. The production of baker's yeast began in the early days of the starter culture technique, which was developed from agar medium cultures or frozen dried cultures. The fermentation medium used for production contains Molasses as a source of carbon and energy sources, which is heated to melt proteins. Sulfides are removed through treatment using acids. Ammonium salts and urea is added to the mix along together with the other minerals ions. pH is set at 4.0-4.4. The aim of this process is to obtain a substantial quantity of biomass, with excellent storage properties and fermentation activities.

ii. The production of single-cell proteins

Today the single-cell protein has been viewed as to be a possible source for satisfying the requirement for protein that is low-cost. Advancements in producing single-cell proteins were noticed between 1960 and 1970. Single-cell proteins are not 100% entirely pure, but it also contains minerals, vitamins, lipids as well as yeasts, algae and bacteria.

There are some advantages to single-cell proteins compared to the plant and animal source proteins. A high yield, high proteins, capacity of single-cell proteins to eat a variety from carbon sources minimal demand for land and production is not affected by seasonal or climatic fluctuations and excellent quality of the product.

Table 4.5.Nucleic acid and protein amount of microorganisms

The industrial production of biomass by microbes can be classified into two major processes:

1. The production of yeast can be utilized in the baking industry

2. The production of microbial cells can be used to make human or animal food

Three major uses for Microbial biomass include:

1. Food fermentation and beverages as well as agricultural uses, biopesticides and mineral leaching

2. Source of food as protein diet. Because they are tasteless and odorless, they can be used in a myriad of food products

3. Fooder for animals

4.3.4. The process involves the creation of Recombinant products by microbes

Because they contain DNA that comes from more than two species, they are also referred to as Chimeric DNA. The DNA of any animal, like either animal or plant DNA can be combined to the DNA from fungi and bacteria to create recombinant DNA molecules. Genes that are of interest could be introduced into microbial cells of other organisms. This method, the recipient could be able to produce homologous proteins. Microbial cells, such as Escherichia Coli and filamentous fungal species may be employed in the production of recombinant substances as hosts. The technology of DNA recombinant is widely employed in biotechnology research as well as in agriculture and medicine.

Recombinant products are created through genetic engineering

Human Growth Hormones

Somatostatin is produced first and inhibits the production of growth hormones. Today, they are utilized for children who are deficient in the production of growth hormone. Human growth hormone comprises 191 amino acids. The host of the growth hormone Escherichia coli that is then fermented using an isolated gene that is later isolated. The growth hormone that is produced in this way is exactly the same as that found in humans.

Human insulin production

Diabetes patients cannot produce insulin. Therefore, the need for an external source to treat those suffering from diabetes. With the help of recombinant DNA technology insulin was created by 1982 using Escherichia coli. There are two approaches to the production of insulin: one from plants, the other from microbes i.e., Escherichia coli.

Interferon

The nasal secretions and our serum can neutralize certain viruses. Certain enzymes, like Acid phosphatase properdin and alkaline phosphatase are the culprits.

Erythropoietin

The kidney produces diverse hormones that are capable of maturation and differentiation in red blood cell within the bone marrow. People suffering from hemoglobinopathies can be treated with erythropoietin by increasing the maturation rate of Red blood cell. The urine of patients who are anemic is a great for erythropoietin. Cloning the hormone gene in the microbe , and then found in Chinese the hamster's Ovarian cells. The supernatant gets purified to be used in the future.

4.3.5. Processes may require modification of Substrates Transformation Process

Microbes alter the structure of chemical substances This process is known as transformation. Microbial cells are able to transform a chemical in order to make it more structurally comparable to economically relevant chemical compounds. Microorganisms could be a catalyst that has stereo-specific positional positioning; the processes that are performed by microbes are much far more exact than chemical processes. In the absence of chemical protection these reactions enable the removal, addition or modification of a wide range of functional groups in precise locations. Catalyzed reactions include Dehydrogenation, Oxidation Isomerization, dehydration, condensation Decarboxylation, Amination Deamination and Hydroxylation. The microbial process has an added advantage over chemical processes because they can be run with comparatively low temperatures and pressures. The most well-known transformation process by microbes is in the production of vinegar.

Chapter 5: Fermentation Technology

5.1. Technology for fermentation

The process of producing microbial products on a massive scale is known as fermentation technology. The ideal conditions for growth are created for the production of desired products by microbial fermentation and they are economically viable on a larger scale.

5.2. Types of fermentation

In general, processes of fermentation can be classified according to the following

1. The fed-batch or batch process

2. continuous/semi-continuous process

5.2.1. Process of batching/fed-batch

In a fed-batch or batch procedure in a fed-batch procedure, the seed culture is inoculated on an environment that contains medium and in the right conditions, cell growth can be performed over a short time with or without the introduction of other nutrients. The end product can be taken at the end of the period of cultivation.

5.2.2. Continuous process

Continuous fermentation, on the other hand, allows substrates to be continually introduced into the fermentor vessels at an appropriate speed, and the final products are harvested in a continuous manner. The majority of current industrial fermentation methods are based on batch/fed batch processes. In the long run continuous fermentation techniques are more efficient in comparison to the batch/fed-batch methods. However, continuous fermentation can come with some weaknesses that include a less concentration of the final product as well as a difficult flow sheets as well as more complicated downstream processing, and the long-term preservation of process sterility.

These complexities are attributable to the difficulties of maintaining main sterility over the lengthy time period of continuous fermentation. In order to allow continuous fermentation processes to be designed for the future industries of fermentation challenges to maintain the sterility for a long time have to be addressed. Elimination in the case of contamination by microbial organisms is essential in all fermentation processes. In order to ensure sterilization, high temperatures and high pressure steam must be used to clean the entire system of fermentation including all pipes, prior to inoculation of seeds.

In the course of the process of growth of cells it is necessary that air be sterilized prior to pumping into vessels. Thus, maintaining the sterility of continuous culture systems is a lot of work energy, equipment, and energy that contribute to the increase in costs of production and the complexity of the process.

5.3. Open fermentation processes

Sterilization can be a very energy-intensive process but nearly all fermentation processes need to minimize the risk of contamination by microbial organisms. The majority of sterilization processes employ steam with high pressure and high temperature to eliminate live microorganisms in the vessels of fermentation as well as the entire pipe system. Thus, the initial capital investment in fixed assets is extremely high , and to a large degree, lowers the competition of the industry. Therefore, it is crucial to design open fermentation processes that don't require the energy-intensive steam sterilization procedure. Open fermentation can lower the amount of capital required for industrial biotechnology, which allows it to compete with other biotechnology.

Certain fermentation methods are being developed to be performed under 'open' conditions. This implies sterilization is not needed since microbial contamination is unlikely. This is a proof of the possibility of performing unsterile (unsterile) fermentation for a long period of time. Here's a brief overview of continuous and open fermentation methods to create a range of important bio-products. The strains that can be utilized to develop of these processes are discussed. Key requirements for the successful implementation of such processes are described. The latest research advances indicate a promising future for continuous and open fermentation in biotechnology for industrial use.

5.3.1. Open fermentation with mixed cultures

In comparison to a pure-culture that is naturally developed, a mixed culture is not dependent on the conditions of aseptic growth, and can therefore be utilized to make industrial bio-fermentations. Some bio-products, including polyhydroxyalkanoates (PHA), lactic acid (LA), hydrogen, and 1, 3-propanediol, were reported to be successfully produced by mixed cultures.

Table 5.1.Examples of open fermentations that have been reported

5.3.2. Open Fermentation methods using thermophilic microorganisms

The thermophilic process employs thermophilic bacteria and are commonly used for LA production. The thermophilic bacteria are able to grow and make LA optimally in a high temperature (at approximately fifty degrees Celsius) effectively preventing the spread of microbial pathogens even in continuous and open conditions.

5.3.3. Open fermentation processes using the use of halophilic microorganisms

Halophilic microorganisms are also extensively studied in process of open-air fermentation. Similar to thermophilic decrease contamination in open conditions. Furthermore, many halophiles make use of low-cost carbon sources like starch, protein or even cellulose. A high concentration of salt can cause corrosion of the equipment and cause damage to the fermentation pipes. Thus, the salt concentration needs to be monitored carefully.

Table 5.2.Difference between fed-batch, batch and continuous-culture technique

5.4. Costs of continuous and open fermentation

Costs for continuous and open fermentation are lower than batches or fed-batch fermentation. The cost of energy, substrate as well as downstream process are the three main expenses associated with operating fermentation. Continuous processes lower expenses for the substrate through recycling them or recycling them. The cost of energy would be decreased due to the absence sterilization. However the cost of processing downstream would not be drastically reduced since it is heavily dependent on the properties of the product rather than the process of fermentation.

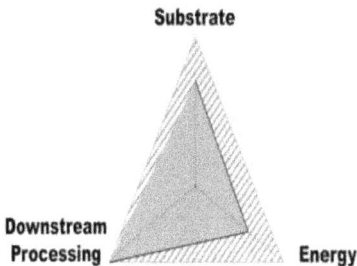

Figure 5.1.Three most significant costs associated with operating fermentation

5.5. Management of processes

The process management is usually focused on:

The initial conditions for the process

Monitoring to determine if the entire process is on the prescribed course

Facilitating manual adjustments to process variables

Deciding when to end the process or take or transfer the finished product

Calculating the thermal and mass balances, kinetics, rate of reaction, yields

Information for statistical records regarding archival and consistent for purposes

Controlling contamination and ensuring hygiene

5.6. The components of the fermentation process

The components of the fermentation process include: as follows:

1. The formulation of the media that will be used in the cultivation process of living organisms.

2. Sterilization of fermenters, fermentation media and other equipment.

3. The process of creating Pure, active culture in order to inoculate vessels for production.

4. The development of the organism during fermentation in optimal conditions.

5. The extraction of the product as well as its removal and purification.

6. The treatment of effluents that are by-products.

5.6.1. Form and Design of Media

In order to determine the most appropriate environment for each individual fermentation process, an in-depth study is required, however any suitable medium has to satisfy certain fundamental needs. Every microorganism requires water, energy sources such as the elements nitrogen, carbon and minerals elements, and perhaps oxygen and vitamins if they are aerobic. It's relatively easy to design an environment at a lower scale that contains pure substances, however the resultant medium might be insufficient for large-scale processes. On the larger scale, you must typically utilize sources of nutrients to make a material that meets the following requirements as far as is possible:

1. The goal is to achieve a minimal amount of unrequested items.

2. It will ensure the highest production rate.

3. It will result in the highest quantity of biomass or product.

4. It is unlikely to cause any problems when making media and sterilizing.

5. It will yield the highest yield of biomass or products per gram of substrate.

6. It is of a consistent quality and will be accessible throughout the year.

7. It should not cause difficulties in other aspects of the manufacturing process including agitation and aeration as well as extraction, purification and the treatment of waste.

It is important to keep in mind, before discussing the development of certain cells in bioreactors and then get them to produce the desired products, that a lot of microorganisms cannot be cultivated employing standard methods. Through molecular genetic research it is evident that there exists a variety of nonculturable cells which means that the cells we grow in our labs is only a small fraction of the population that has been that is adapted to rapid growth generally in media that are rich in nutrients at temperatures of around 37 degrees Celsius (+/- 20 degrees Celsius).

The fermentation process concentrates on the rare exceptions. The usual methods of operation for the bioreactor or fermenter is the inoculation of pure culture and maintaining a monoseptic state during the entire process. This isn't the typical condition of the majority of microbiota. In the laboratory or in an industrial setting microorganisms, plants, insect and animal cells develop on nutrient solutions that contain all the elements they need to develop and produce the secondary or primary products that the cells have been created to produce. These solutions of nutrients are known as media. It is crucial to select the appropriate medium used for laboratory research as well as industrial bioprocessing if one wishes to get the most of the costly and time-consuming investment made to develop the microorganism strain or cell line that is being used. The choice of the appropriate medium could be the difference between the research project or industrial process.

Medium design is an easier process, but it is frequently complicated by issues such as the cost, the transportation of components, the availability of substrates, the reliability of the substrate source and handling, storage convenience of storage and preparation, in addition to security and health issues that are increasingly essential in our current environment. It's difficult to overlook that the most important issue is how to provide microorganisms and cell line with the supply of nutrients that are needed in an easily accessible form. In a perfect world, every component of the medium would easily dissolve in water, making them accessible for the cells. Many media, especially on an industrial scale, do not conform to those ideal circumstances and have suspended solids and oil which complicate the process of the sterilization process and fermentation operation.

Types of Microbiological Culture Media

Media may be semi-solid, solid, or liquid. In this publication, solid and semisolid media won't be examined as liquid media; only those used to process biomaterials will be discussed. The majority of liquid media can, obviously, transform into solid media with the inclusion of an appropriate gelling agent such as agar or gellan. Be sure that the gelling agent is completely dispersed and dissolving prior to attempting for sterilization of the medium.

The bioprocessing-related media that are used are divided into three categories based upon their composition:

i. Synthetic

ii. Semi-synthetic

iii. Complex

i. Synthetic Media

Synthetic media are chemically defined. The components are all recognized as is the exact amount of each. These media are typically quite basic, consisting of the energy source of carbon as well as a nitrogen source as well as a range of salts (usually organic) However, when the cell line selected is extremely meticulous or requires specific requirements for growth the complexity of the media could be significantly increased.

Synthetic media are a good choice for research and laboratory settings where precision in experiments is crucial and data interpretation has to be precise. In general, these media are more expensive than other types of media particularly when certain ingredients like vitamins and the growth factor are needed since these components can be expensive when they are supplied in their in their pure form. Cell yields tend to be lower than when the same line of cells is grown in semi-synthetic or complicated media. It is, naturally it is easier to study the effect of one or two nutrients on cell growth and physiological processes using these media than more complicated ones. Such media are generally fully soluble and provide the fewest downstream processing challenges in an industry context or purification/recovery challenges in a small laboratory context

ii. Semi-synthetic Media

Semi-synthetic media are generally chemically defined, namely synthetic, but may also contain one or more unspecified component(s) with a variable however controlled, like yeast extract, which is especially useful when cells require the use of a variety of B vitamins. These media are beneficial for research and lab circumstances where a specific organism requires a particular substrate which is expensive to provide in its pure form on a regular basis. These components can also be useful in situations where the particular nutritional needs aren't well-known and are a good source of different nutrients, such as yeast extract is utilized in a shotgun-based approach to providing small amounts of nutrients. Fish, animal, plant and microbial extracts are all that have used for a long time to provide nutrients and growth factors for particular organisms.

iii. Complex Media

Complex media consist mostly of materials that are generally from animals or plants and are of unclear and varied composition. The composition of these materials varies in batch after batch and the composition of each is influenced by the place of origin and the time of year and minor changes in the methods of production. The availability of seasonal products can vary significantly. They're generally inexpensive and are available in bulkquantities, and the source must be reliable. Complex media are employed in various biotechnological processes, particularly those that yield high volume products that are low in value, e.g., single-cell protein (bakers yeast). It is uncommon to employ these types of substrates at the research stage unless an industrial process is being replicated precisely in the research lab.

Medium Components

1. Carbon Sources

Carbon sources are essential for the cell to have energy and the substance to develop. The average microorganism contains around 50percent carbon which makes carbon the most important substrate. Care should be exercised to make sure the carbon content does not be limited. The biomass yield on carbon is about 0.5 This implies that if a biomass level of 50 gL-1 is required, then 100 gL-1 from carbon must be provided, but not always in a single step.

The Glucose-based molecule is appropriate for the growth of all cell lines, no matter if it's plant, animal, or microbes. It is available in a powdered pure form. The substrate is easily accessible and reliable, it is easily stored as well as easily handled. It is not a significant threat to health and security. These attributes make glucose a sought-after carbon sources. One method for supplying glucose at a greater scale is using sugar syrups that are made from an hydrolysis process that breaks down starch. The major benefit of the use of glucose syrups is their price, since it is considerably less expensive as powdered glucose.

Sucrose Sugar - The most popular sugar in laboratories for research usually sucrose. It is used by a variety of however, not by all types. Sucrose is available commercially in various types and grades, from pure granulated forms , to complex Molasses solutions (above). Sucrose doesn't tend to have the same problems like glucose. Although it can be subject to caramelization when over sterilized, it can be autoclaved/sterilized with nitrogen compounds without the same problems as glucose.

Lactose is a type of sugar. Lactose is only utilized by certain types of cells, e.g., Escherichia bacteria, and it is not metabolized until extremely slowly. Sugar is only useful for certain commercial processes that rely on the complicated substrate whey, an by-product in the milk industry that is a mixture of lactose and.

Additional Sugars Other sugars could be utilized as substrates, but are usually very specific to the selected type of cell, e.g., melibiose can be used to create yeast cells.

Sugars that fall into this class are too costly to be used regularly. When choosing a unique sugar that is not in the regular category, the main questions to be asked are the following: 'Why do we need this sugar to be used?' What benefit does the organism get from it from it?'

Oils - A variety of oils are employed to create carbon sources for the bioprocess industry. Oils from rapeseed (canola oil) and methyloleate are two of the most well-known options. They both contain carbon as well as an energy source, the oils are affordable and readily available. The plants that produce oils are able to grow across a variety of climate zones and are easily cultivated, ensuring that supply is reliable. There are variations in the composition and the quality of the oil, and the oils must be periodically examined for variations in the content of components among batches. In a laboratory, need to be considered to ensure that the proper conditions for storage (4 degree Celsius) are in place.

2. Nitrogen Sources

The nitrogen content of any medium determines the amount biomass that can be produced for the specific cell line, provided there is plenty of carbon readily available and all the nutrients needed are in the initial medium. Nitrogen is essential for the growth and the synthesis of, for example proteins, nucleic acids, and so on. The form and source vary. Certain nitrogen sources can be provided as a benefit in conjunction with the inclusion of more complicated nutrients.

The most common nitrogen sources include

Ammonia is often utilized for industrial purposes, but it isn't an often-used source of nitrogen employed in research laboratories due to of the high volatility of liquid and its handling issues. Health and safety concerns are an actual risk associated when using this nitrogen source and careful consideration is required when it comes to the preferred substrate. Storage reservoirs, special handling devices and breathing apparatus are all needed, along with additional precautions in case of any leaks. The benefits of using ammonia are that

* It easily dissolves in the medium.

It is immediately accessible to the phone

It is also affordable (although the equipment for storage and handling could not be)

Nitrogen-based Salts The salts are Nitrogen-based. Ammonium Sulfate $(NH_4)_2SO_4$ ammonium chloride, NH_4Cl are the most common nitrogen sources that can be discovered within the scientific literature. Ammonium is highly utilised by many species and using the salt is a cost-effective and effective method of supplying cells with the nitrogen it needs.

Other Substrates

Elements - Many elements are necessary for the development of microorganisms. Each one must be supplied usually by way of an inorganic salt to allow the cell to develop and function effectively.

Trace elements - They are considered micronutrients that are only required in very small quantities, in most cases mg per Liter. The roles of trace elements inside cells are diverse and varied , but they are usually related to enzyme activity. Common trace elements are iron (Fe which is probably one of the most essential elements due to its importance in the process of respiration within cells).

* Copper Cu

* Cobalt, Co

* Manganese, Mn

* Molybdenum, Mo

* Chromium, Cr

Growth factors

Growth factors, such as trace elements, can be used in small amounts by cells. They are often produced within the cell. However, certain cells are unable to create certain key growth factors that are required to be supplied to cells through the medium. They are usually organic compounds, like purines, vitamins, pyrimidines along with amino acids. These compounds are typically expensive to include in the pure form, and it's more common for bioprocessing to utilize an alternative that might contain less pure but can meet the needs of the cell. Vitamins are among the most frequently utilized cells' growth factors in media. Supplying these in yeast extracts or other animal and plant extracts is inexpensive and easy to use.

Inhibitors

Every medium formulation must be free of substances that have been proven to block the development of the cell. However, many cells, when fed excessively and deprived of nutrients, may exhibit unwanted behaviors and could release harmful waste products or toxic byproducts which can cause slower growth or the production of product or the cessation of the process itself.

5.6.2. Sterilization of fermenter, media and all other equipment

Fermentation products are produced through the growth of certain organisms within a nutrient-rich medium. It is mandatory to have seed cultures free of contamination throughout the entire process, from initial culture through the fermenter for almost every fermentation process. The fermenter can be sterilized through either the removal of the viable microorganisms using the use of physical methods, i.e., filtration or by degrading the microorganisms by using a deadly chemical, such as heat radiation, or chemical.

The elimination of contamination, and for the development of a specific microbes can be achieved through:

(i) Utilizing a pur inoculum to start the process of fermentation.

(ii) (iii) Sterility inbound and outgoing air

(iii) The medium is sterilized that is to be used

(iv) Infusing Sterilization into the vessel used for fermentation.

(v) Sterilizing any materials in the process, to later be added into the ferment

(vi) Aseptic conditions throughout the process of fermentation.

(vii) The construction is appropriate for the bioreactor/fermenter for sterilization and the prevention of contamination during fermentation.

Figure 4.1.Fermentation Process

A. The sterilization of media culture

When they are first prepared in the beginning, nutrient media have many different vegetative cells as well as spores within the medium for cultivation, water, as well as the vessel. The media must be cleaned of any inappropriate methods prior to inoculation. There are a variety of methods available to sterilize, however heating is the most commonly used method. There are a variety of factors that affect the effectiveness of sterilization by heat, i.e., the quantity and kind of microorganisms in the environment and their pH as well as what is the chemical composition in the medium and the size of suspended particles. Vegetative cells are eliminated rapidly with a moderate temperature, for instance, 60 degC for 5-10 mins However, to ensure the elimination of spores temperatures of 121 degrees C are required to last for 15 mins.

Filter sterilization is usually used for all the elements of nutritional solutions that are heat-sensitive. Vitamins, sugars or blood components, and antibiotics are examples of heat-labile elements which require sterilization through filtering.

The majority of nutrient media are sterilized in batches in the bioreactor with 121 degC. The time for sterilization can be calculated based on the characteristics of the medium as well as the dimensions that the fermentation unit. In addition to the nutrient media but also the electrodes of the fermenter, fittings and valves have to be sterilized. So, the actual times for sterilization should be determined empirically for the specific solutions of nutrient within the fermenter, and are considerably longer than the calculated times. Smaller fermenters can be sterilized using an autoclave. However, larger fermenters are sterilized using directly or indirectly steam injection.

B. The sterilization of the fermentation air

The majority of fermentation processes run with high aeration and the air that is supplied to the fermenter has to be cleaned. The amount of microorganisms and particles in the air can vary greatly based on the air's location, movement, and prior air treatment. In general, outdoor air contains 10 to 100,000 particles per cubic meter and 5-2,000 microorganisms in a micrometer. In all, about 50 percent are fungus spores and 40% are Gram-negative bacteria.

Fermenters typically work with Aeration rates of 0.5-2 the vvm (air volume/liquid volume per minute). The options to sterilize gases include heating, filtration, gas Scrubbing gas injection (ozone) along with radiation (UV). Of these the two, only heating and filtration are viable.

C. The construction is appropriate for the fermenter

There should be a few gaps in the fermenter to ensure the sterility of the fermenter is maintained. Larger openings and smaller openings should be sealed by using O-rings or gaskets that are flat. If a shaft with a moving part enters the wall of the fermenter specific issues of maintaining sterility should be resolved.

If foreign microorganisms intrude into the fermentationprocess, then the following outcomes could occur:

i. The medium could aid in the growth of the organism producing it as well as the contaminant. This would result in an increase in productivity.

ii. The foreign organism can cause contamination to this final item. For instance, single-cell proteins cells, after separation from the liquid, make up the final product.

iii. If the fermentation continues in the meantime, the contaminant could outgrow the organism that is producing it and obstruct the process.

iv. The contaminant can affect the final product's quality which is common in the case of bacterial contamination during antibiotic fermentations, where the degrading of antibiotics is a typical resistance mechanism. In addition, the contaminants would be insensitive to the usual inhibiting effects that the antibiotic has.

V. The contaminant can create compounds that can make the subsequent removal of the product challenging.

5.6.3. Active culture production

The process of developing an inoculum has specific requirements that must be followed to create an inoculum. Before inoculating the culture the fermentation, it must meet the following requirements:

i. It should be free of contamination.

ii. It must have an ideal morphological structure.

iii. It should retain its capabilities of forming products.

iv. It should be in an active and healthy state, which will reduce the duration of the lag phase of the fermentation.

v. It must be accessible in sufficient quantities to ensure an inoculum that is of the ideal size.

The general structure of a process called fermentation is as the following:

"Stage 1: preservation of the inoculum

"Stage 2: the inoculum building-up

* Stage 3: fermenter culture

Stage 1: Preservation of Inoculum

The goal for preservation should be to preserve the strains for as long as is possible with no cell division. The most effective method for preservation should be developed for every strain. Three methods are the most frequently used:

Frozen storage (-18, -80 or -196degC)

Storing at lower temperatures (2-6degC)

Lyophilization

Storage temperatures between 2 and 6 degrees Celsius are the most vulnerable; there is a high chance of contamination and reverse change due to frequent transfer. The storage of frozen samples is extremely frequent, and frozen samples could be kept for a number of years. The amount of survivors is vital due to the fact that the majority of microorganisms are destroyed during freezing and freezing and subsequent thawing. The most efficient method of preservation of strains is to use that of Lyophilization (freeze-drying).

Stage 2: Growing of the inoculum

The culture that is preserved is revived by the growth of an Erlenmeyer flask that is placed on an organic shaker or solid medium (if the formation of spores is required). The second batch of shake culture is generally produced in larger flasks in order to ensure sufficient inoculum is available that can be used in small-scale fermenters. From lyophilized strains inoculum growth can take between 4 and 10 days. In frozen cultures, the development of inoculum can take up to 448 hours for bacteria and 1-7 days in the case of fungal growth. In refrigerated culture, the growth of inoculum is 4-24 hours for bacteria , and 1-5 days for fungi.

3. Stage 3: Fermenter culture

The nutrient medium for production should be optimized, not just in the ingredients used , but also in the method by which the media is prepared and sterilized, the pH before or after sterilization. The most crucial parameters to consider in the process of fermentation process include:

Temperature

Aeration

Stirring

Figure 4.2.Fermentation Process

5.6.4. The development of the microorganisms in the fermenter

The efficiency of fermentation is contingent on the quality of the biomass and its creation under defined environmental conditions. To reach this end it is essential to know what happens to the fermentation process and how to create ideal operating conditions. Therefore, temperature, oxygen concentration of the media, its pH level, level of agitation and other variables should remain in check throughout the process.

Illustration 4.3.Process of Fermentation

The products produced during the fermentation process comprise various secondary and primary substances that are created during the upstreaming process. As we all know, the primary metabolites are microbial compounds produced during the exponential phase of growth. Their production is an essential component of the normal process of growth. They are intermediates and final product of the anabolic pathway which lead to the creation of monomers that are utilized by cells to build up the building block (amino acid and nucleotides) to make polymers (protein and DNA) and coenzymes (vitamins). However, the catabolic pathways' primary metabolites (citric acid as well as acetic acid and alcohol) do not have biosynthetic origins however are vital for growth since they are linked to energy production, utilization of substrates and balance of redox.

Industrially speaking, the most important principal compounds are organic acids, amino acids, vitamins nucleotides, as well as solvents. They are produced by a wide variety of fungi and bacteria. They are used in a variety of applications within the pharmaceutical, food chemical, nutraceutical and chemical industries. A large portion of these metabolites are made by the process of microbial fermentation, not chemical synthesis since the processes are competitive economically and generate bioactive isomers. Numerous other essential chemicals for industrial use can be produced through Microbial fermentation (glycerol and other polyhydroxy alcohols) but they are being produced inexpensively using petroleum by-products. But an increased interest in fermentation of ethanol by microbial organisms organic acids and solvents has initiated as a result of increasing prices of crude oil.

Secondary metabolites of microorganisms and plants are generally low-molecular weight natural substances that are not vital to the existence and growth of the organisms that produce them, however, they play a role in the interactions between organisms and their surroundings. It is widely believed that secondary metabolites originate from primary metabolites that have numerous and distinct biological functions.

There are many of secondary metabolites that are commercially used for human health products such as food products, agricultural chemicals, industrial biochemicals, and nutritional supplements. They include antibiotics, antiviral and anti-tumor agents, cholesterol-regulating drugs, pigments, flavors, fragrances, toxins, effectors of ecological competition and symbiosis, pheromones, enzyme inhibitors, immunomodulating agents, receptor antagonists and agonists, pesticides, and growth promoters of animals and plants. The amount of synthesis from these secondary compounds may be affected by a variety of elements, including the nutrition, the growth phase growth rate, molecules and feedback control, the conditions of cultivation (temperature and pH light, temperature, and dissolved oxygen) as well as physical microenvironments.

Typically, the majority of these second-products are made at a minimal level in the initial strains that produce them, since they are "secondary" in the microorganisms' living processes and plants. The production level is less than what is required to produce commercially, creating a problem to meet commercial demands. This has led to small successes in commercial production of goods through plants.

However, microbial fermentation technology is established with numerous commercially successful products that are used in a variety of applications in the food industry, pharmaceutical industry, agricultural industry biofuels and chemical industries and the environmental industry. However, these commercially viable microbes are just tiny fraction of the vast array of secondary metabolites produced by microorganisms in both aquatic and terrestrial environments. In order to develop a reliable industrial process to produce any useful product produced using microbial fermentation and cultivating plant cells It is crucial to identify an superior strain or cell line and effective processing strategies which can accomplish the followinggoals:

1. Stable and consistent product yield and productivity in low-cost processing conditions

2. The highest conversion rate of the most affordable substrates available

3. Specificity and high product selectivity aids in downstream purification.

5.6.5. The extraction of the product and purification

The removal and purification of the final products could be difficult and expensive. The ideal is to create a top-quality final product that has a rapid recovery rate as fast as is feasible with minimal investments in plant, and at minimal expenses. However, the recovery costs of microbial products can range from just 15% to as much 70 percent of total manufacturing expenses. The selection of the recovery method is dependent on the following parameters:

1. The amount of the final resultant product is determined by the concentration of the broth used for fermentation.

2. The extracellular or intracellular location of the microbial substance

3. The chemical and physical characteristics of the item (as an aid in selecting methods of separation)

4. The intended usage of the product

5. The minimum acceptable standard for purity

6. The amount of bio-hazards in the broth or product

7. The impurities that are present in the broth of the fermenter

8. The marketable price of the product

5.6.6. Treatment with effluent

Each plant's fermentation process uses raw materials, which are then transformed into different products. Based on the specific process, different amounts of a variety of waste materials are generated. Common wastes comprise unconsumed organic and inorganic media components like Microbial cells, as well as others suspended solids filtration aids, waste from cleansing processes such as cooling water, waters that contain trace amounts of alkalis, acids, human sewage, solvents, etc.

It was once common to dispose of waste directly onto a suitable land-based area or into an adjacent watercourse. This cheap and simple disposal method is not feasible, nor is it eco-friendly. Due to the expansion of industries and the growing population and a greater awareness of the damage caused by pollution the need for the treatment and control of waste hasgrown as well as will increase. Water authorities as well as other similar organizations are more involved in fighting pollution due to industrial and domestic wastes. Additionally, the legislation in all countries that are developed currently regulates the disposal of waste.

Typically, the fermentation effluents contain harmful substances that directly impact the aquatic fauna or flora. However, the majority of wastewaters do contain high levels of organic matter. They can be easily oxidized by bacteria and will drastically reduce the dissolved oxygen content (DOC) of the water in which it is absorbed, in the absence of a significant diluting factor.

Chapter 6: Therapeutic Applications Of

Enzymes

6.1. The therapeutic application of enzymes

There are various kinds of therapeutic enzymes which have various types of uses. They are used for anticoagulants, thrombolytic or oncolytic as well as to treat metabolic disorders. Therapeutic enzymes are usually available in lyophilized forms in pure formulations. They are also available with bio-compatible buffering sodium or Mannitol as a diluting agent. In the case of urokinase, it is a human urine, and is used to break blood clots. Proteolytic enzymes can play an important job for anti-inflammatory properties.

The main uses of therapeutic enzymes are for treatment of cancer, as well as other illnesses. In the treatment of acute lymphocytic leukemia the asparaginase enzyme exhibits an extremely promising impact. It is able to inhibit the production of amino acids that are not essential such as L-asparagine. The asparaginase enzyme doesn't affect normal cells. Since normal cells are able to synthesize the enzyme in sufficient quantities to satisfy their needs However, they trigger significant decreases in the exogenous free concentration that this enzyme produces. In this manner, the condition of starvation is created , to which tumor cells are vulnerable. Glutaminase is an antitumor treatment for Leukaemia and accomplishes this function by converting L-Glutamine into L-Glutamate. The enzyme is responsible for the decrease in levels of L-Glutamine within the bloodstream.

Table 6.1.Some important therapeutic enzymes and their uses

6.1.1. Collagenase to treat damaged skin

Collagenases are the only enzymes which break the peptide bond in collagen. Certain bacteria make collagenases. e.g. the Clostridium species as well as Vibrio species. It's also made by cells in the body. It's part of the immune system's normal response. The synthesis of collagenase enzyme is stimulated by Cytokines. They stimulate different cells, including osteoblasts and fibroblasts for producing this enzyme. This is how they contribute to indirect tissue destruction. They are responsible for the hydrolysis of collagen in resident tissues. They have a specific action and do not have an impact upon other protein. Collagenases have been extensively used to treat burns and dermal ulcers. They play a crucial role in healing wounds by taking out dead tissue and dead skin that it's applied to.

6.1.2. Hyaluronidase as a treatment for damaged tissues

It can be used effectively to treat heart ailments. It triggers the hydrolysis that results in the breakdown of Hyaluronate and is efficient in treating heart attacks. It prevents the formation of scar tissue, the expansion of the heart, and the thinning of the heart's walls. It relieves the discomfort and stiffness of the heart muscles. It also aids in the healing of burns, and skin lesions. It also helps to prevent the effects of ageing. Vibrilase TM is an enzyme that is photolytic. It is derived by bacteria like Vibrio proteolytic. It was found to be extremely effective against protein distortion. For example, proteins that have been denatured are found in burnt skin. Chondroitinases is the enzyme that are used to heal the damaged spinal cord. When they work they eliminate the glial scar and begin the process of healing nerve tissue. It was discovered that the hydrolytic function of Hyaluronidase shares a similarity with chondroitinases based on chondroitin-sulfate.

This means it could help repair wounded nerve tissue.

6.1.3. Lysozyme to treat infectious illnesses

Lysozyme is an enzyme which functions to act as an anti-bacterial mediator. It is antibacterial in nature and is extensively used in the treatment of bacteria-related infections. It accomplishes this function by breaking down the layer of peptidoglycan. This is an important part that forms the wall of cells for nearly all bacteria. It has been discovered that it provides a strong defense against various bacterial infections. This is why it has been utilized to treat of septicemia and bacteremia. Lysozyme activity is also observed in infections caused by viruses, such as HIV. For instance, RNase A and RNase U (urinary) both eliminate the viral DNA. Chitinases are a different antimicrobial agent that is found naturally. Chitin is found within the cell wall of a variety of microbes that cause disease. Examples include protozoa, helminths, and fungi. Chitin is a great option for antimicrobial agents of various kinds. The lytic enzyme derived from the bacteriophage line is used extensively against different bacteria that cause infections. It targets specifically walls of cell membranes of different bacteria like Bacillus anthracis Streptococcus pneumonia and Clostridium perfringens. The lytic bacteriophages can be extensively used to treat a variety of illnesses. Therefore, they are effective against new resistant bacterial strains to drugs.

6.1.4.   Asparaginase.   glutaminase. chondroitinase to treat cancer

Asparaginase can be used as an antitumor drug to treat Leukemia. It does this by converting L-Aspargene into L-Aspartate and renders it inaccessible to cancerous cells. In the treatment of acute lymphocytic leukemia the asparaginase enzyme is an extremely promising result. It is able to inhibit the production of non-essential amino acids , such as L-asparagine. Asparaginase does not have any impact on normal cells. Since normal cells are able to produce this enzyme in sufficient amounts to meet their needs, they result in a substantial reduction in the exogenous free quantity that this enzyme produces. This is how an unfavorable starvation condition is created , which makes cancer cells are vulnerable. Glutaminase is utilized as an anti-tumor drug to treat Leukaemia and accomplishes this function by converting L-Glutamine into L-Glutamate.

In recent research, it has been discovered an enzyme called arginine degrading (PEGylated arginamine deaminase) has a role to play in the prevention of human malignant melanoma. It is also effective in the fight against hepatocellular carcinomas. Recently, a novel PEGylated enzyme called Oncaspar1 has proven effective to treat children suffering from newly diagnosed acute lymphoblastic leukemia.

Chondroitinases are enzymes that have been utilized to regenerate the damaged spinal cord. When they work they eliminate the glial scar and begin the process of healing for nerve tissue. The enzyme is transported by a monoclonal antibody which is specifically designed for cancer cells. It eliminates cancerous cells by activating the drug to become active. It doesn't affect on normal cells.

6.1.5. Ribonuclease is an antiviral agent

Ribonucleases are often abbreviated as RNases. They are part of a group of enzymes called nuclease. It breaks down the RNA into smaller pieces. Ribonucleases can be classified into two categories: exo-ribonuclease and endo-ribonuclea.

* Endo-ribonuclease can either cleave single-stranded or double-stranded RNA in accordance with the class that the enzyme belongs to.

* Exo-ribonuclease breaks down RNA by eliminating the nucleotides that are terminal. This can be accomplished by removing 3 or 5percent of RNA.

The enzyme is extensively used as an antiviral medication in the treatment of viral illnesses. It results in an hydrolysis process of viral DNA. It blocks the replication of viruses via catalytic activity , and dimerizes viral DNA. It blocks the function of the M2 channel protein and blocks viral uncoating. Additionally, it inhibits the neuraminidase enzyme and neutralizes the viral antigen. This is then removed by the immune system of the host.

6.1.6. Lactamase is used to treat of allergic reactions

B-lactamases are enzymes natural produced by a vast range of microorganisms. Different species of bacteria produce these enzymes. For instance, Staphylococcus aureus Haemophilus influenza Neisseria gonorrhoeae, among others. The enzyme is susceptible to B-lactam medications. It does this by breaking the b-lactam the ring that is found in these medications. It's used to treat allergic reactions caused by medications that include cephalosporine, penicillins monobactam, carbapenems and cephalosporine. The allergic reactions that are triggered by these medications are of type 1 where immunoglobulin E plays a role, and hypersensitivity type 1V that involve t-cells. The hypersensitive reactions can be serious and can be fatal. B-lactamases relieve the allergic reaction by converting penicillin to penicillate.

6.1.7. Utilization of urokinase or streptokinase to break up blood clots

Streptokinase, an extracellular enzyme. It is made by various strains of streptococci, and is utilized in clinical studies as an intravenous thrombolytic drug. Blood clots can form because of any injury. If they are not treated, they could create life-threatening and serious problems. They may cause obstruction of blood vessels. When this happens, the tissue can die because of oxygen deficiency. Streptokinase can be utilized to break down blood clots through the conversion of plasmaminogen into plasmin, and then breaking down fibrin and blood clots called thrombin.

Urokinase is part of the serine proteases class. Urokinase can be employed to break down blood clots through the conversion of plasmaminogen into plasmin, and breaking down fibrin and the thrombin clots. This action is carried out by activating extracellular blood coagulation matrix components such as fibrinogen and prothrombin.

6.1.8. Trypsin to treat digestive inflammation

Trypsin is digestive enzyme, and is part of the class of proteolytic enzymes. It is secreted by the pancreatic and trypsinogen cell in the digestive system. It can be involved in degrading of proteins. Tissue repair mechanisms are composed of four phases: hemostasis, coagulation Proliferation, and remodeling. If inflammation continues it can lead to swelling, pain, and production of pus. The inflammation is relieved by trypsin hydrolysis of proteins. It prevents the undesirable destruction of proteins in cells and helps to eliminate the sign and signs of inflammation caused by injury to the tissue. It also provides an analgesic impact.

6.1.9. Utilization of uricase in the treatment of joint diseases

Urate oxidase enzyme or uricase is not found in human beings. It is responsible for the oxidation process of uric acids and results to the creation of 5hydroxyisourate. The subsequent hydrolysis of 5-hydroxyisourate results to the formation of the allantoin as well as CO. Uricase enzyme is predominantly found within the liver. It is present in the form of a tetramer. Each tetramer is composed of identical subunits. Each subunit has two copper binding sites.

Uricase enzyme extracted in A. Flavus contains the 301 residues that are utilized to treat gout which is a condition of joints. The cause of this disease is an excessive accumulation of urates crystals. In the course of treatment, Uricase results in the oxidation process of uric acid/urate oxidation to 5hydroxyisourate (allantoin) and eliminates symptoms and signs of Gout.

6.1.10. Serratiopeptidase for the treatment of blood vessels

Serratiopeptidase is a member of the proteolytic enzymes class that are produced by non-pathogenic enterobacteria like

Serratia species. The bacteria were isolated from the intestines of silkworms. Because of its proteolytic action it leads to the degrading of fibrin blood clot-controlling factors. It also causes the breakdown of denatured proteins and cell debris. The enzyme has also been utilized to reduce inflammation. It has also been utilized to combat atherosclerosis. Atherosclerosis is a condition that affects blood vessels. Atherosclerosis is not only the hardening, but also the thickening of blood vessels occurs and can cause heart issues if left untreated. To prevent heart problems it is recommended to cut down on consumption of fats during this disease. This enzyme breaks down the vessels' thickening by taking away the plaque that is formed inside the arteries.

6.1.11. Papain for digestive problems

Papain is mostly found in natural fruits such as Papayas. Enzymes like Papain are taken orally after eating food to treat digestive issues. They aid in digestion. The geriatric disorder is a gastrointestinal disorder and is usually associated with old age. In this condition there is a decline in the digestive system takes place. This is why an insufficient or low production of digestive enzymes takes place. This is the reason how the system of digestion is unable to process food efficiently. In these cases, sufferers are afflicted with various issues like malnutrition, constipation, and constipation.

6.1.12. Bromelain is an anti-inflammatory drug

Bromelain is one made up of protease enzymes. They are found naturally in different components and fruit of pineapples. They have been utilized for tropical healing to eliminate dead tissue and proteins that have been denatured from skin burns. Bromelain and papain are being used to help tenderize the texture of milk. Bromelain is also used as an anti-thrombolytic as well as anti-inflammatory agent for the treatment of cardiovascular diseases.

6.2. Iso-enzymes

Iso-enzymes are two or more enzymes that have different structures, yet identical in their purpose. There are a variety of similar enzymes, that are able to perform similar biochemical processes. Examples include Creatine Kinase as well as LDH. Iso-enzymes differ in physical and chemical properties, i.e., kinetic properties, electrophoretic mobility amino acid composition along with amino acid sequence.

There are two major kinds of isoenzymes.

Functional plasma enzyme

Non-functional plasma enzyme

6.2.1. Plasma iso-enzymes that are functional and not.

A few enzymes, their pro enzymes and their respective substrates, are present in blood circulation throughout the day. They perform various physiological functions in the bloodstream. Some functional plasma enzymes are Lipoprotein lipase and Pseudocholinesterase, which are usually secreted from the liver. However certain enzymes exist in plasma that are not associated with any purpose in the blood circulation. It appears that these non-functional plasma enzymes might arise from the normal destruction mechanisms. These processes are typical for common destruction of leukocytes the erythrocytes, as well as many other cells. Any type of tissue damage or necrosis because of injury or illness is typically responsible for the elevated plasma levels of various non-functional plasma enzymes. The table shows specific iso-enzymes and the reasons for their elevated plasma levels.

Table 6.2.Examples of Isoenzymes that are commonly tested to determine the diagnosis

6.3. Medical applications of lipases

Lipases are enzymes that hydrolyze lipids. They break down the fats into fatty acids as well as Glycerol. They are taken from fruits that are naturally occurring like avocados. Lipases were also isolated from microorganisms referred to as Galleria mellonella. They have shown bactericidal action against Mycobacterium tuberculosis which is the wild type strain H37Rv. The initial studies were conducted to determine the presence of promising new sources of medicines. Lipases are also employed to treat digestive disorders. Lipases are also used to treat cancer. In this process, they are involved in activating the tumor necrosis factors. Gastric lipase , a human-derived enzyme, has a high degree of stability. It is regarded as to be a viable tool in treatment with enzyme replacement therapy. This is why they are extensively used in the treatment of digestive disorders. The lipase that is isolated from Candida rugosa is utilized for the production of the drug lovastatin. It's effective in decreasing the levels of cholesterol in the blood. The lipase that is isolated of S. marcescens plays a role in the production of a substance called diltiazem chloride. It is used primarily to treat coronary vasodilation.

6.4. Enzymes in the diagnosis of diseases

Enzymes are organic substances that are naturally soluble catalysts. They are naturally component of living cells, and possess specific actions. They are "protein in nature" and are inactive when temperatures drop below 0 degrees Celsius. They are heat-labile and thus destroyed when temperatures rise above 100 degrees Celsius. Enzymes are found in various organs. They are also present in various types and in different locations. They can also be utilized as reagents in a variety of Bio-chemical measurements and estimations.

Organs with different enzymes like kidneys liver, heart, and muscles of the skeletal system are released into bloodstream in the case of diseases. The measurement of the related enzyme levels at low or high levels in blood can indicate particular disorders. For instance, a skewed Creatine Kinase levels signify that the muscle is weak and injured.

Polymerase Chain Reaction (PCR) is extremely useful to diagnose various genetic disorders at the prenatal period. The disorders that are affected include Huntington's Disease sickle cell anemia, and thalassemia. The table below lists the different enzymes, their locations and significance in clinical practice.

Table 6.3.Examples of enzymes typically assayed to detect a problem

6.4.1. Assay of enzymes for the detection of acute myocardial infarction.

The World Health Organization (WHO) has defined criteria for identifying acute-myocardial ischemia. The criteria include signs of pain in your chest, changes in ECG results, as well as elevated levels of biochemical markers related to myocardial damage. Research has shown that in half of patients, those who exhibit "typical" symptoms are not suffering from AMI. On the other hand biochemical indicators show a remarkable ability to diagnose AMI. The biochemical markers include aspartate transaminase (AST), creatine phosphokinas and troponins, as well as myoglobins and lactate dehydrogenase. Creatine phosphokinase is found to have normal values of between 170 and 24 IU/L for females, and between 24 and 170 IU/L in males. It converts creatine to the phosphocreatine that provides energy during contraction of muscles. CK is present in large quantities in skeletal and heart muscles. It's also present in tiny amounts in the brain. However, it is not found in kidneys or the liver.

6.4.2. Enzymes associated with liver diseases diagnosis

The liver is a crucial organ. It is a crucial part of the human body. It is situated anatomically to the left side of belly and it plays a role in detoxification of substances. The liver also produces a distinct protein, which is responsible for blood clotting, as well as in other functions. But, there are different Serum testing for the enzyme are accessible to determine the presence of liver disorders. These enzymes are usually divided into two groups that are grouped. The elevated levels of one group of enzymes signifies an injury to the cells of liver while the other group's serum levels that are elevated indicate the presence of cholestasis.

6.4.3. Enzymes to screen for liver damage

The increase in aminotransferases is an extremely precise and vital indicator for determining liver cell damage. This is extremely helpful in the detection of acute hepato-cellular diseases, including liver disease. These are aspartate-aminotransferase abbreviated as AST and an Alanine-aminotransferase abbreviated as ALT. At different concentrations, AST has generally been found in the liver, the cardiac muscle, skeletal muscles and kidneys, as well as the brain as well as pancreas, leukocytes lung, and erythrocytes. The normal serum concentration is around 0-41 in IU/L. They usually appear in serum at low levels. However, their concentration increases in the bloodstream significantly when there is damage to the liver. If you suffer from acute viral hepatitis (VIH), their levels could rise up to more than 1000 IU/L.

6.4.4. Enzymes that reflect the presence of cholestasis.

5'-nucleotidase and the alkaline-phosphata found within or near the tubular spaces within liver cells. The tubular spaces are typically filled with the bile released by live cells. Gamma-GT is found in the epithelial cells of the bile-duct epithelial cell. It is also found in the endoplasmic retina. The high levels of three enzymes include alkaline-phosphatase, g-Glutamyl transpeptidase abbreviated as GGT 5'-nucleotidase and the presence of cholestasis. The normal serum concentration of alkaline phosphatase is between 0-45 IU/L.

A slightly elevated amount of this enzyme could be seen in patients who are over 60. The normal serum is full of different iso-enzymes found in various organs. They are found primarily in the liver, the placenta and bones, as well as in lesser amounts in the intestinal tract. It plays a role in the movement of amino acids through membranes. It is primarily found inside the kidney, the biliary duct of the pancreas, as well as the liver. Enzyme activity could be a trigger in the case of alcoholism. Certain drugs can trigger its activityand increased GGT levels are seen in jaundice with obstruction. GGT levels are moderately elevated in the case of hepatitis. When there is obstruction to the biliary system, high levels are detected.

6.5. Amylase estimation

Amylase is an enzyme for hydrolyzing starch. It breaks down starch into various sugars. Amylase is present in the human body and other mammals saliva. It is the first step in the process of digestion. Amylase is also found in a few natural fruits, such as bananas and mango. Banana is also a source of the glucosidases. If they are found in higher than normal amounts within the body, it could result in a number of medical conditions. These conditions include acute pancreatic inflammation as well as peptic ulcer and the torsion of an Ovarian cyst. In all the body the measurement of amylase levels in fluids have a significant clinical value. It is found in the peritoneal fluid, urine, and other fluids in the body within the normal range. Ab-amylase activity detection in different body fluids is of great clinical importance These conditions include diabetes, pancreatitis, and research into cancer.

6.5.1. Clinical Significance of the Enzyme Estimation

Estimation of enzymes is of great clinical importance for diagnosing of various illnesses. The estimation of enzymes aids in the early identification of diseases. It also assists in determining the likelihood of developing a disease, and to determine the drug's reaction to a specific disease. The estimation of enzymes can help identify the duration of the illness.

Chapter 7: Enzyme Applications In The Txtile

Industry

7.1. Enzymes in the textile processing

The process of processing textiles using enzymes has numerous benefits. The use of enzymes makes the process not only green but also enhances the product's quality. Research has shown that just 75 enzymes are employed in the process of making textiles. The primary enzymes that are used to the industry of textiles comprise oxidoreductases as well as hydrolases. The enzymes that belong to the hydrolases group comprise cellulases, amylases and proteases as well as pectinases and lipases. Amylases have been utilized within the industry of textiles from the 1980s onwards. These enzymes have a long-lasting significance and are utilized to de-size fabrics following weaving. Cellulases are employed to remove fuzz and fibrils fibers. The proteolytic enzymes are extensively used to get rid of scales on wool fibers. They provide an improved anti-felting capability. Esterases are employed for an incomplete hydrolysis process on synthetic fibers and not just enhance the hydrophilicity of these fibers, but they assist in finishing the process. Catalases are efficient in removing H2O2 from the fiber after bleaching. Therefore, it reduces the consumption of water. The table below illustrates how different enzymes are used in the industry of fabric.

Table 7.1. Applications of enzymes in the fabric industry

7.2. Amylases's role for the fashion industry (de-sizing)

Amylases are part of the class of enzymes that trigger the hydrolysis process of starch. They produce various products like dextran, as well as smaller glucose polymers. Amylases can also be classified according to the kind of sugar produced by Starch hydrolysis. Examples include a-amylase as well as b-amylase. Alpha-Amylases are produced by a variety of microbial species, like yeasts, fungi and bacteria. However, the enzymes that are commonly used in industrial settings were isolated from filamentous bacteria and fungi.

Amylases that are of fungal and bacterial sources are quite stable between pH 4 and 11. The ideal temperature for Alpha-amylases ' activity is typically dependent on the microorganism that it is produced. The ideal temperature for their activity could be between 25 and 130 degc according to the growth rate of the microorganism that produces them. The thermostability of their cells can be improved with the addition of calcium. Following weaving, not just the sizing agents, but also the non-cellulosic material naturally present in the cotton must remove from fabric. This is essential to prepare the fabric for the next step of finishing and dyeing.

In the beginning, de-sizing was performed using alkali, acid, or various agents for oxidation at high temperatures. This chemical process had several drawbacks. It was not entirely effective for the removal of starch that later affects not just the dyeing process , but also leads to the degrading of the fibers. This also affects the natural softness that cotton provides. Today, enzymes like amylases are gaining popularity instead of de-sizing using chemicals. Because they are extremely efficient and specific in their actions they totally remove the sizing material , thereby avoiding any harmful effects on fabric. Through the enzymatic process, starch transforms into dextrin, a water-soluble substance. Then, it is removed by washing.

This process is not just more environmentally friendly in comparison to chemical treatment, but also improves the working environment.

7.3. Pectinases function in the industries of the textile (enzymatic scouring)

Pectinases is the name given to enzymes that trigger the breakdown of Pectin and other compounds. Pectins are polysaccharides with complex structures that are found naturally within the cells of plants and form a part of the central layer. Pectinases are part of the complex group of enzymes that carry out the task of breaking down of the pectic substance. They are mostly produced by pathogens and saprophytes of plants found in the natural world. Pectinases-producing organisms could be fungi or bacteria that remove the cell wall from plants. The enzymes for degrading pectins are divided into three main categories, and they comprise

* Polygalacturonases

* Pectin esterases

* Polygalacturonate Lyases

Pectin esterases were created predominantly by a broad range of plants. The plants include bananas, citrus fruits and tomatoes. However, they are also produced by various microorganisms, such as bacteria and fungi. This leads to the degrading of pectin's methyl-esters, and results in the production of pectic acid. Pectate lyases are used to aid in bio-scouring.

7.3.1. Scouring process by using enzymes

Cotton that is raw or coarse contains many non-cellulosic adulterations. These impurities comprise pectins waxes, hemicelluloses, and mineral salts that are found in cells of fibers. They give hydrophobic properties to raw cotton. Therefore, they greatly interfere in aqueous chemical processes on yarns, including dying and finishing. Therefore, prior to the efficient dying process, getting rid of the impurities is essential since they hinder the dye binding process. This is why the process known as Scouring significantly improves the ability of fabrics to be wettable. The majority of scouring processes are done with alkalis, like sodium hydroxide. However, chemical treatment comes with certain disadvantages. For instance the chemical can have an adverse effect on the cellulose. This causes not just an increase in strength of the fabric, but also diminution in the fabric's mass.

Additionally, wastewater produced contains a higher salt level, BOD and COD. Through enzymatic bioscouring, cellulosic structure remains in good shape. Thus, enzymatic processes prevent cellulosic weight loss , and increases the strength. Numerous enzymes, such as cellsulases and proteases, pectinases and lipases/cutinases in combination or as a single unit are used to aid in research on the bioscouring of cotton in various research. It was discovered that pectinases work the best than the rest.

7.4. Cellulases play a role for the fabric industry (denim finishing)

Cellulases break down compounds through hydrolysis. They result in the destruction of cellulosic materials into smaller components like oligosaccharides which then transform into glucose. Cellulase activity occurs through an array of at least three enzymes that work synergistically. Endoglucanases (endocellulases) are enzymes that break bonds that are internal to the chains of cellulose found in the amorphous zones. Cellobiohydrolases are exocellulases that cleave bonds that are formed between the crystal edge of the cellulose chain. They produce primary cellobiose. In this manner,

Cellobiohydrolases are synergistic not just with one another , but also with endoglucanases.

It is for this reason that a combination of these three enzymes will have more activity than the combination of individual enzyme separately. Cello-biose as well as other soluble oligosaccharides can be further converted into glucose through the enzyme beta-4-glucosidase. Additionally the enzymes are commonly produced by fungal or bacteria. The most important species with the creation of enzymes include Penicillium Trichoderma, Penicillium, and Fusarium. Cellulases can be used at temperatures that range from 30 to 60 degc. Cellulases were first utilized in the textile industry through denim finishing as early as the 1980s. Today, they are efficient in the treatment of yarn as well as different cellulosic fibres.

7.4.1. Denim finishing with enzymes

A variety of clothes receive an washing treatment that gives them the appearance of shabby. Like stone-washing of denim jeans. This process removes the blue-denim color has been discolored due to the roughness of pumice stones rubbing against the cloth surface. With the help of cellulases, the stones used in the industry of textiles related to jeans could be decreased or removed. Therefore, there's less damage not only to machines, but also to the fabric. This will also decrease the amount of pumice dust in the environment of the laundry. The productivity can also be improved as laundry machines will hold more clothing and will have less stones. There are various kinds of cellulases readily available and each one has unique characteristics. They can be used separately or together to create a distinct appearance. The endoglucanase created by Trichoderma Reesei is highly effective in the removal of the color. It gives a high-quality stone washing effect, even with the lowest level of hydrolysis. Then, a brand new gene-modified strain T. Reesei was created to make endoglucanase, a compound with high activity.

7.4.2. Pilling and fuzz elimination using enzymes

Cellulases are utilized extensively to remove the fuzz and pills. In the field of textiles there are many different types of cellulases. Natural but also synthetic cellulosic yarns can be removed through enzymatic actions. This process of enzymatic improvement to enhance the performance of yarn is often known as bio-polishing. The primary advantage of the treatment is the reduction of pilling. The pill is actually the form of a ball of fuzz which can be seen upon the surfaces of fabric. They can impact the quality of clothing as they create an unattractive and knotty appearance of the fabric. Cellulases eliminate the microfibrils (fuzz) by expanding from fabrics' surface. Because they are more susceptible to enzymatic activity, through these processes, the microfibrils are less durable. This is why they are prone to split off from the fiber's surface and the surface of the yarn gets smooth. So the elimination of fuzz provides a soft more smooth and smoother feeling, as well as greater brightness of color.

7.5. Serine proteases' role (pre-treatment of wool)

The majority of the time, Subtilisins belong to the category of alkaline serine proteases made by various Bacillus types. They break down ester and peptide bonds through the formation of an intermediate known as an acyl-enzyme. These are made in the form of a pre-proportion precursor. A prepeptide that is amino-terminal which is a signal-peptide is composed of 29 amino acids. The peptide is the one responsible for elimination of pro-subtilisin from the plasma membrane. Pro-peptide fragments are composed from 77 amino acids. It's located between the pre-peptide as well as the mature sequence. It is referred to for its intramolecular chaperone. It plays a crucial role in the proper folding of active enzymes that are mature. Active site the enzyme is composed of three distinct types of amino acids called aspartate, histidine and serine.

7.5.1. Wool treated with enzymes

The natural hydrophobic nature of wool in Crude Wool is since the epicuticle membrane is not just made up of fatty acids , but also other hydrophobic impurities like wax and grease. The use of strong chemicals is typically used to eliminate them. This method is also known as alkaline Scouring. This is because in this procedure it uses different chemicals that are mostly alkaline i.e. sodium carbonate, potassium permanganate salt, sodium sulfite, as well as hydrogen peroxide-based compounds. Wool fibers shrink when the process that is wet. The most efficient commercial method of preventing shrinkage known as chlorine Hercosett method was invented over 30 years ago. It is highly effective method because it provides a high-quality anti-felt effectwith minimal damage as well as less loss of weight however it does have some major disadvantages. They include poor handling quality as well as a lack of durability, the discoloration of fibers, troubles during the dying process and a negative environmental impact due to the release of absorbable organic Halogens.

To avoid the drawbacks of chemical treatment that chemically cause problems, subtilisin proteases were employed in numerous studies to replace chemical pre-treatment agents for wool. Numerous studies have shown that pretreatment of wool using proteases improved anti-srinkage characteristics, reduced adulteration as well as the affinities of later dyeing. Because of its small size this enzyme has the capacity to enter the cortex of fibers and cause damage to the internal portion of the wool's configuration. In the future, the size of the enzyme was increased through chemical crosslinking using glutaraldehyde, or by attaching synthetic polymers, like polyethylene-glycol. This way the amount of enzyme infiltration is decreased.

7.6. Cysteine has a role to play in the industrial textile process (silk degumming)

Cysteine proteases (CPs) have been extensively utilized to break down the amide, peptide ester, thiono-ester and thiol-ester bonds. There are more than twenty kinds of cysteine proteases to be identified. The enzymes are further divided into exopeptidases such as cathepsin, carboxypeptidase B and X and endopeptidases like papain, cathepsins, ficain and bromelain. Exopeptidases break down peptide bonds close to the N- or C-terminals on the substrate. As opposed to endo-peptidases, they dissolve bonds of peptides far from the C or N terminals. To activate an enzyme the pro-peptide that is located at the N-terminus is required to break down. The peptide also plays a role as a blocker of enzyme. Papain is one of the most powerful recognized cysteine protease. It was isolated by the fruits of a plant called Carica papaya around 1879. It is the first protease with a crystallographic structure. Papain has the highest activity from the pH range of 5.8 up to 7.0 and at temperatures between 50-57 degrees when casein is the primary substrate utilized. Papain is a natural substance with broad specificity due to its ability to cut a variety of peptide bonds.

7.6.1. Degumming process for silk

Papains are used extensively to boil cocoons as part of the degumming procedure of silk. Silk that is not refined requires degumming in order to rid it of sericin. It is a proteinaceous material that covers the fibers. Degumming is typically done making use of alkaline solutions that have soap. These kinds of harsh treatments can also harm fibrin's structure. Many acidic, alkaline or neutral proteases are used as degumming mediators to degumming. Most importantly the proteases, alkaline proved to be the most effective in removing sericin. The alkaline proteases can also improve silk's structural characteristics like the shine the handle, softness, and shine.

7.7. Transglutaminases (TGS) to treat wool

Transglutaminases are widely utilized in the process of processing wool in the textile industry. They have been discovered to enhance several characteristics of silk, including shrink resistance, handle wet capability, softness, Tensile strength retention, as well as dye uptake. They also reduce the amount of the tendency for felting. The enzyme treatment also shields against the harm that is caused when using typical detergents. Transglutaminases fall under the category of the thiol enzymes. They are responsible for the post-translational modification of proteins mainly through the process of causing crosslinking between proteins and proteins. They also perform this activity by lipid esterification, polyamines covalent-conjugation, or the de-amidation of glutamine residue. Transglutaminases have been identified from a range of animals, plants, and bacteria . They were initially identified from the microbial genera Streptomyces mobaraensis. The enzyme is released by an active enzyme, which transforms into an active, mature form through the action of two enzymes that are endogenous. This mature form of enzyme is characterized by a molecular weight that is 38 kDa. It is the only cysteine residue called Cys-64 located at the catalytic location.

7.8. The role of laccases in bleaching and decolorization

The laccases in the body are exocellular proteins. They use molecular oxygen to oxidize phenol as well as other non-aromatic and aromatic substances. They mostly belong to blue multicopper oxidases, an enzyme family. Laccases naturally occur in bacteria, plants, and even insects, but mostly within fungal organisms. Laccases are widely employed to neutralize the color of effluents by the industry of textile. They are able to degrade dyes with various types, as well as synthetic dyes. Laccases are utilized as an environmentally friendly tool for the treatment of dye wastewater. They are commonly employed for fabric bleaching. Laccases' bleaching process of yarn creates the appearance of white due to the removal of natural pigments. The majority of bleaching for industrial purposes is carried out with hydrogen peroxide that is nearing boiling temperatures. The elevated temperature as well as the alkaline pH are extremely harmful to fibers.

However large water resources are also required to eliminate hydrogen-peroxide out of textile. Laccases are responsible for increasing the whiteness of yarn through the process of oxidation that flavonoids undergo to create compounds. Exchange or grouping of chemical bleaching with an enzymatic bleaching system results in reduced fiber damage , and reduces water consumption.

7.9. Catalases function in the textile industry to treat bleach liquor

Catalases (CATs) typically hydro-peroxidases, play a role in the breakdown of H2O2 as well as the production of O2 and water. The catalases were made by various bacteria, including bacteria and fungi. Catalases are also extracted from animals (bovine liver) that are typically cheaper than other. There is a way to make affordable catalases that are microbial in origin by using low-cost recombinant techniques with specific properties such as thermos-stability and pH stability. In the industry of textiles bleaching is usually done using H2O2 following the de-sizing and scouring processes but prior to dying. A reducing chemical was utilized to reduce the hydrogen peroxide previously. However, now this is accomplished by making use of catalases to degrade H2O2. Catalases are not just able to eliminate the need for reducers, but have also decreased the requirement for rinse water. This means that there is less polluted water as well as a significant decrease in the use of water.

Chapter 8: Enzymes And Applications In The

Feed Industry

8.1. The presence of enzymes in feed for animals

Enzymes are chemical catalysts that are released by cells to enhance certain chemical reactions. This term refers to the enzymes released by the digestive tract that assist with digestion of food. Nowadays, these enzymes can be produced and added to feed for animals. Hydrolyzing enzymes typically increases the nutrition value of animal feed. These include Xylanases Proteases, Glucanases, and Phytases. The production of animal feed involves high temperature (65-95degC). This is because mesophile enzymes suffer a massive loss of activity. Three kinds of enzymes i.e. the phytases, carbohydrase, as well as proteases are usually considered to be useful in the industry of feed.

8.1.1. Phytases

The primary substrate for the phytase enzyme is phytic acid which is the type of phosphorus stored in the tissues of plants. The phytic acid is a problem for animals due to it binding mineral amino acids that can be a problem for

120

animals. The binding causes the expulsion of nutrients that are beneficial to the environment, leading to an impairment in performance.

Phytases have been incorporated into monogastric diets for over 10 years. According to the previous article the principle of action and the primary objective of phytase is the reduction of excretion of phosphorus. Its effectiveness continues to increase due to the savings in cost of diet. The first savings concern with the reduction of dietary phosphorus costs However, nutritionists also have the ability to decrease amounts of soy meal because of increased digestibility of amino acids.

It is a well-proven technology to lower the cost of feed through reducing the use of inorganic phosphorus and reducing excretion of phosphorus in manure. The process works by releasing some of the phosphorus that is not digestible (and additional nutrients) that are typically found in feed ingredients, and making the nutrients available for the purpose of productive use.

8.1.2. Carbohydrase

Carbohydrase enzymes can enhance the amount of energy that can be obtained from ingredients in feed. The most important carbohydrase enzymes are amylase and xylanase. They help to improve the digestion capacity of carbohydrates in feed ingredients.

The improved digestion increases the amount of energy within the small intestine, which helps increase growth as well as other processes of production. Corn accounts for a large portion of energy in the typical diet of poultry.

* Xylanase generates power from the fibrous component of grains as well as by-products from grain. It shatters the arabinoxylan structure found in corn or wheat, allowing animals to take in the components of it to provide energy sources. This is a limitation on the amount of additional fat or energy that is required in food.

Amylase (also known as Amylase) is a starch-digesting enzyme that assists in the digesting of more starch in corn. Amylase improves starch digestibility which means it can provide more energy.

They function in the stomach to break down as well as break up carbohydrates, such as

122

fiber, starch, and non-starch polysaccharides to simple sugars, which give energy to animals. Sources of grain like wheat, corn and barley are coated with hard coatings on their exteriors. The majority of the coating was broken down when feed mill processing began however, it is not totally. The fibrous coating of grain cell walls is not digestible and between 10 and 20 percent of it is able to pass through. Carbohydrases can attack and destroy these starchy grains molecules.

8.1.3. Proteases

Protease is a digesting enzyme for proteins that breaks down the storage protein chains that are bound by starch in the feed ingredients. This makes the energy derived from starch that is bound to proteins available to birds to be used for productive tasks. Proteases are also able to remove protein anti-nutrients that are that are found in foods such as soybean. The function of proteases is to make proteins easily accessible.

Raw ingredients that have low digestibility for amino acids show the highest response to an external protease, which is why it's so important when using alternative ingredients for food purposes. Proteases can help feed producers reduce the nutritional risks that come with the quality of feed and make use of the best feed ingredients available.

The enzymes do not have to be restricted to diets that contain other ingredients. Animals who eat a traditional soybean-corn diet are not able to utilize 100% protein. Thus, adding protease the diet of soybean-corn meal will increase the digestibility of amino acids, and consequently improve the performance of animals.

8.2. Enzymes for polysaccharides that are not starch-based

Non-starch polysaccharides include a vast range of polysaccharide molecules being among the most characteristic compounds in the cells' wall. They are either soluble or insoluble when in water.

Oats and barley are both rich in b-glucans. They is the reason for the lack of nutritional value in the diets that are based on these basic ingredients. Supplementing feed with b-glucanases reduces the polymerization rate of B-glucans, which allows for more efficient utilization of nutrients that are released, resulting in an increase in the intake of feed and a decrease in efficiency of conversion to feed.

Arabinoxylans are the major source of non-starch polysaccharides soluble that are released from wheat, rye and triticale. Similar to this xylanases are able to depolymerize this substance and increase the nutritional value of this substrate.

8.3. Why should we use enzymes in feed for animals?

Feed is usually the biggest expense for animal production. Pigs and poultry do not consume 15 to 25% of their food.

* Young animals are born with an immature digestive system, so enzyme production might be insufficient.

Feed ingredients typically have antinutritional elements which are why pigs and poultry do not have enzymes required to disintegrate these nutrients.

Table 8.1.Enzymes utilized in the feed industry for animals

8.4. The requirements for enzymes that are included in feed

The enzymes used in animal feed must:

* safe and simple to handle

* stable during storage

* effective and active for the animal

* stable at temperatures up to a certain point attained during the process of making feed

* compatible with vitamins, minerals and other ingredients for feed.

* Free-flowing to ensure that the feed is thoroughly mixed throughout the feed

8.5. Beneficial effects of the use of animal feed enzymes

A mixture of amylase, protease and xylanase enzymes work to attack the digestible parts of feed ingredients to boost the amount of energy available for growth and egg production. The inclusion of these enzymes in the diet is usually combined.

Increase efficiency and decrease cost by breaking down non-nutrients, allowing the animal to digest food more effectively.

* Improved consistency - - reduce the variation in nutrition of ingredients in feed, resulting in more consistent feed and better animal performance.

* Energy availability increases the amount of energy available for chickens by 3 to 5 percent.

* Aids in maintaining the balance of gut health - by improving digestion of nutrients, which means that lower levels of nutrients in the gut may cause the growth of harmful bacteria.

* To ensure a healthier environment, proteases and carbohydrase may help to decrease nitrogen output, while phytotase can reduce the excretion of phosphorus.

Table 8.2.Microbes utilized to make commercial enzymes

Figure 8.1. Mechanism of Action of some feed enzymes

Chapter 9: Enzymes Replaced In Other

Industries

9.1. Enzymes that are used in laundry products.

Amylases, proteases Cellulases, peroxidases, and proteases are all used to make laundry detergents. The enzymes are found in nature, however the most recent advances in the use of protein engineering are being employed to design superior enzymes to be used in this process.

9.1.1. Serine Protease Subtilisin

Subtilisin is subject to numerous mutations to investigate and alter its folding and catalytic mechanisms as well as its stability, activity and the substrate's specificity. Stability and activity are enhanced in the presence of detergents, and even those that have oxidizing conditions.

Stability improvement the susceptibility of subtilisin to bleaches derived from oxygen has been reduced by replacing the methionine residue close to catalytic serine by alanine since the oxidative bleach attacks methionine, and inhibits enzymes.

Activity Improvement: the activity of subtilisin depends on calcium. Calcium sequesters that eliminate calcium from the body are reduced through increasing the affinity Ca for the enzyme. This is also possible by adding more negative charges near Ca binding sites. Also, calcium-free subtilisin mutations are made.

9.1.2. Lipases

Lipases can be active at the interface between water and substrate. Surfactants that hinder the in the adsorption process of lipases on the interface are able to inhibit hydrolysis of the substrate. Therefore, the stability of lipases in detergents is enhanced by a variety of methods.

An anionic compatibility with surfactants of the cutinase was diminished by the introduction of more positive charges on the protein's surface. In contrast, the addition of negative charges produced an enzyme that was more stable with anionic surfactants.

9.1.3. a-amylase

A-amylase is an isolated enzyme from the natural world, is sensitive to oxygen bleach, and its resistance can be improved employing techniques of genetic engineering.

9.1.4. Cellulases

The activity of alkaline and the compatibility with detergents of cellulases are also enhanced by making use of the most recent methods.

9.2. Hydrolysis of starch and manufacturing of fructose

Producing fructose from starch is an massive industrially significant process.

Starch Oligosaccharide Glucose Fructose

The process includes some of the enzymes listed below:

i. a-amylase(pH : 6, 90-95degC, + Ca)

ii. Glucoamylase(pH : 4.5, 60degC)

iii. Glucose isomerase(pH 7 60degC, +Mg -Ca)

The ideal scenario is that the entire process can be accomplished in one step However, in actual practice the process is carried out in three distinct steps due to the distinct requirements for each enzyme.

9.2.1. a-amylase

The enzyme needs a very high temperature of pH 6 and requires calcium to function in addition to these conditions, but they are not needed for the next enzyme (Glucoamylase). Therefore, the efforts of engineering have been focused on the production of the a-amylase that can work in the absence of calcium and can have a lower optimal pH.

9.2.2. Glucoamylase

In this case, thermostability and reaction efficacy are the main targets for improvement. Thermostability has been improved through Mutagenesis, and a reduction in the production of by-products has been accomplished by re-designing active sites.

9.2.3. Isomerase for glucose

The thermostability and the activity of this product under acidic conditions were enhanced by the site-directed mutation.

9.3. Xylanases in the Pulp industry

The Xylanases enzymes are employed in the process of bleaching pulp for getting rid of the lignin in turn, reduce the amount of chloride chemical. Pulp produced by chemical pulping can be hot as well as alkaline. The enzyme can reach temperatures of as high as 90degC and pH levels of more than 10.

Therefore, the goals of enzyme engineering are thermostability and high alkali along with an increase in activity under these conditions. Thermostability and enzyme performance has been enhanced, however, the tolerance to alkali needs improvement.

9.4. Chemoenzymatic synthesizing

Utilizing enzymes as biocatalysts is a field with huge potential. The enzymes can take a variety in complex molecules for substrates they exhibit chiral as well as specificity for enantiomers. They only have some by-products, and do not call for lengthy blocking and deblocking processes.

However, many times, enzymes don't remain stable in a reaction mix with organic solvents. Therefore, the ability to tolerate organic solvents, their stability and the improvement of catalytic activity are the main goals in protein engineering.

Chapter 10: Products For Medical Use, And

Applications Of Biotechnology

10.1. Pharmacogenomics

It has been discovered that individuals suffering from the same condition often react differently to treatment because of different gene expression. Tumor Suppressor Genes - regulate oncogenes. Oncogenes are genes that create proteins that can serve as transcription factors or receptors for growth and hormone factors. They are also enzymes that are involved in a array of ways to alter the cell's growth characteristics that cause cancer.

BRCA1 (or 2 increases the likelihood for developing cancer in the breast However, there are different breast cancer cases that do not exhibit this type of inheritance, and must be treated in a different manner (i.e. and with different treatments)

10.2. Nanotechnology and Nanomedicine

Nanosensors are able to measure the levels of hormones and blood pressure as well as unblocking arteries. They can also detect and eradicate cancerous cells.

10.3. Artificial Blood

The first blood tests were conducted in the 80s to detect HIV. But, it's not available in the poorest, developing countries. There is a need for secure blood and cell-free solutions that contain molecules that can bind and transport oxygen. replacements for blood, i.e., Hemopure which is made from cow hemoglobin.

10.4. The use of vaccines as well as Therapeutic Antibodies

Vaccines boost immunity. There is also a possibility that vaccination can be effective against ailments like Alzheimer's disease, or addiction to drugs. Antibodies are also employed in certain types of therapies like the creation of Monoclonal Antibodies.

10.5. Regenerative medicine and Gene Therapy

The growth of tissues and cells can be used to repair or replace organs and tissues that are damaged for example, in treating cystic fibrosis. The defective cystic fibrosis ' transmembrane conductance controller (CFTR) is typically used as a pump within the cell's membrane, allowing the electrically charged chloride atoms of cells. If cells aren't able to eliminate chloride then they absorb water in an attempt to lessen the concentration of chloride inside the cell. This results in thick and sticky mucus.

10.6. Transplantation of Tissue and Cells

About around 50,000 Americans are diagnosed with Parkinson's disease each year. This condition is caused by the loss of dopamine-producing neurons deep within the brain. This causes shaking, balance issues and weakness, as well as loss of dexterity and muscle rigidity and inability to swallow. It can also cause diminished sense of smell and speech issues.

Fetal tissue grafts may be able to treat this condition. The idea is to implant fetal neural cells to establish an association to other neurons. More than 100 patients have had transplants and have seen some improvement.

10.7. Autograft

8 million procedures are conducted every year, and around 4000 patients die waiting for surgery. Autograft is the process of transferring a patient's tissue from one part in the body into another. For instance a vein

that is located in the leg is utilized in coronary bypass. However, all organ transplants happen between people and require a check to ensure compatibility. Histocompatibility complex of more than 70 genes that make tissues typing proteins must be compatible. There are a variety of MHC proteins (one group is known as human leukocyte antigens, or HLAs) which have been treated with immunosuppressive drugs however there are issues.

10.8. Therapeutics for cells

It is the process of using cells to replace damaged tissues to release crucial biological molecules. The process of encapsulating living cells into miniature plastic beads are known as biocapsules. The capsule is designed to protect cells from rejection, but allows the chemicals to spread out. It is currently being utilized for Type 1 diabetes therapy.

10.9. Tissue Engineering

The replacement of tissues and organs through the cultivation of these in a skin graft or culture have been developed successfully up to now. In general, 8 to 12,000 bases pair unit of 5'-TTAGGG-3'. The lifespan of cells is influenced by telomeres i.e. when cells divide, the telomeres shrink, which leads to the process of senescence (aged cells). Telomerase repair telomere lengths by adding DNA nucleotides to cover the telomere following each round that a cell divides.

10.10 Stem Cell Technologies

The CDC estimates that the number of Americans suffer each day from illnesses that stem cell technology could be able to treat in the future. Adult-derived stem cells can do everything embryonic stem cells do , and eliminate the ethical question of dismembering embryos. Such as amniotic-fluid-derived stem cells and reprogramming somatic cells.

Chapter 11: Composites Biotechnological

Process Of Drug Induction

The hierarchy for biotechnological manufacturing. The initial stage of development. Subsystems that are of the type bioobject - bioreactors biomass separators, extractors and more.

The second phase of construction. Consolidation of subsystems to create a functionally unifying chain (site and workshop). The technological basis for the development of standard block-modular solutions. The third step of construction is the sequence of modules and blocks of functional zones. Experimental-industrial installation, the enterprise of the finished cycle. Auxiliary and basic (general engineering) subsystems.

The process of implementing successive phases of transformation of the raw material into a medical product. Optimizing the bioobject the process and device for biotechnological manufacturing.

Preparations to be used for the creation of micro-biological objects. Multistage preparation of seeds. Inoculators. Kinetic curves of the growth of microscopic organisms within closed systems. Rate of change of the amount of microorganisms present in this exponential growth stage to the number of cells within the system.

The nutrient media are complex and synthetic. Their constituents. Concentration of an non-renewable component of the nutrient medium , and how quickly the organism reproduces within the technological niche. The Mono equation.

Methods for sterilizing the nutrient medium. Criteria of Dandorfer, Humphrey. The preservation of biological integrity of media after sterilization. Sterilization of equipment for fermentation. "Weak points" inside sterilized containers. Issues with sealing equipment and communication.

The cleaning and sterilization process of the process air. Plan of preparation for the flow of air that is delivered into the fermentation unit. Cleaning preliminary. Sterilizing filtration. Limits of the dimensions of the particles transmitted. The efficiency of the filter. The coefficient of breakthrough.

The criteria for selecting fermenters for the achievement of specific goals. Biosynthesis classification based on technological parameters. The principles of organization of the flow of materials periodic, semi-periodic Otemno-top, continuous. Deep fermentation. Mass exchange. Surface fermentation.

Conditions for the fermentation process are based on the physiological significance of the product to the producer . Primary metabolites, secondary metabolites molecules with high molecular weight. Biomass as a product of target. Conditions for fermentation with recombinant strains to form target products that are alien in relation to biological objects [66

Purification, isolation, and concentration of biotechnological substances. Specific characteristics of the first phases. The process of sedimentation in biomass. The equation of precipitation rates. Coagulants. Flocculants. Centrifugation. Isolation of cell culture liquids from higher plants, microorganisms and. Separation of the targeted products transformed into a solid phase. Separation of Emulsions. Filtration. Initial treatment of the liquid to achieve a better phase separation. Acid coagulation. Thermal coagulation. The introduction of electrolytes.

Methods to extract intracellular proteins. The destruction of cell walls of biomaterials and extraction of the desired products.

Ion exchange chromatography and sorption. Affinity chromatography is used to identify of enzymes. Membrane technology. Classification of to separate membranes. The broadness of the methods used for purifying the product of biosynthesis and organsynthesis at the very end that they produce (from concentrated substances). Drying. [6]

Standardization of the medicines obtained through techniques of biotechnology. Packing.

2. RECEPTION OF ANTIBIOTICS

Antibiotics are particular products with vitality, with significant physiological activity to certain microorganisms, as well as to malignant tumors that stop their growth or completely inhibit the development of malignant tumors (NS Egorov 1979). Some of these compounds with a total of is in the vicinity of 5000, are approved to be used in medical. The following classes are the most significant antibiotics for therapeutic value (Table 1.).

The classes of antibiotics mentioned above don't end their variety Their list of antibiotics is updated each year. Reasons for unending focus on the need for new antibiotics as evident from Table. 10, are correlated with the potential toxicity of the existing antibiotics, allergic reactions triggered due to them. They also result in the rise in resistant microorganisms that cause pathogens against the antibiotics and additionally, the need to discover methods of combating pathogens against which currently available antibiotics aren't effective. The most common search routes comprise:

1. Test new products. Since the start in the 80s, myxobacteria which produce a lot of antimicrobial substances are being studied.

2. The chemical modification that antibiotics undergo. Antimicrobial macrolides can be harmful to humans. For instance, heptane amphotericin B, which is used to treat vital signs in mycoses that are severe is a cause of irreparable kidney damage. Amphotericin methyl ester, which are less harmful and still retaining antifungal action, were found. Immobilized enzymes can be used to modify the penicillins as well as cephalosporins.

3. Mutasynthesis. Mutant strains are utilized to block the synthesis of parts of an antibiotic's molecule are inhibited. Analogues of these fragments are added to the medium of culture. The microorganisms use these analogues for biosynthesis which results in an altered antibiotic.

4. Engineering of cells. Hybrid antibiotics can be made by using, for instance, innovative combinations of aglycon and sugars.

5. Genetic engineering introduces into genome of microorganisms of the details of the enzyme that is necessary to modify the antibiotic produced for instance, its methylation using methylases [66.

Table 1 important category of antibiotics for therapeutic use (for IG .. Egorov 1979, D.Lanchini, Parenti F 1985)

Class Common antibiotics Producers Who are they the drug affecting? Mechanism of action - Difficulties in the therapeutic use

B-Lactam Penicillins, Cephalosporins, Mushroom delivery Renicillium Cephalosporum The Gram-positive bacteria and the Gram-negative ones Disturbance in cell wall production Allergy reactions

Aminoglycoside Streptomycin, gentamicinand kanamycin tobramycin, amikacin, Actinomycetes from the Genus Streptomyces, Micromonospora bacteria genera. Bacillus The general rule is Gram-negative bacteria irreversible inhibition of protein synthesis impact in the nerve of the auditory as well as kidneys

Tetracyclines Antibiotics that have similar names Actinomycetes from the genus Streptomyces Gram-positive, negative gambling bacteria, rickettsia and protozoa, chlamydia Reversible inhibition of protein synthesis. Distribution of resistant strains

Macrolides antibacterial erythromycin Antiprotozoal, antifungal Polyenes Actinomycetes from the Genus Streptomyces Similar Gram-positive bacteria as Mushrooms and some protozoa

The plasma membrane is disrupted. Toxicity

Polypeptides and depsipeptide polymyxins, Bacitracins, gramicidins and bacitracins from generally, Gram-negative bacteria mechanism of action differs The high toxicity

The most important goal is to improve the effectiveness in the biosynthesis of existing antibiotics. It was possible to achieve significant results through the years of selecting producer strains by induced mutagenesis as well as stepwise selection. For instance, the production of Penicillium strains on the production of penicillin was has increased between 300 and 350 times. There are a variety of possibilities regarding potential cloning of genes in these "bottlenecks" that are involved in biosynthesis of antibiotics or when all biosynthetic enzymes are coded with one operon.

An approach that is promising is the treatment of antibiotics particularly their incorporation into Lygusomes. This permits patients to deliver the drug to specific organs and tissues, which increases the effectiveness of the drug and minimizes adverse negative effects. This technique can also be applied to other medications. For instance, kalaazar is a condition caused by leigma can be treated using antimony medications. However the dose that is therapeutic for these drugs is harmful to human beings. The composition of liposomes and antimony compounds, they are delivered selectively to the organs that are affected by leishmania including the liver, spleen and spleen.

In lieu of an antimicrobial being present in our body its creator and antagonist, a cause of the disease can be introduced. This idea is derived from the research that was conducted by II Mechnikov on the suppression of putrefactive microflora within the large intestines of humans by the lactic acid bacteria. A key factor in the development of dental caries appears to be that of the mouth-resident bacteria Streptococcusmutans It releases acids that damage teeth enamel, as well as dentin. A mutation of Strept is now available. Mutans, which when injecting into the mouth, almost does not produce corrosive acids and displaces the pathogenic wild species and produces a protein that can be fatal to it.

3. OBTAINING HORMONES

Biotechnology offers medicine with innovative ways to obtain valuable hormones. Significant shifts have been observed over the last few years with regard to the synthesis of the hormone peptide.

Growing Hormones in Biotechnology

In the past, hormones were extracted from tissues and organs of both animals and humans (donor blood from organ surgeries or cadaveric material). It took a significant amount of materials to produce an insignificant amount of hormone. Thus, the human growth hormone (somatotropin) is derived from the pituitary gland of the human and each pituitary gland has less than 4 mg. However approximately seven mg of somatotropin each week is necessary for a child who is suffering from dwarfism. The treatment plan should last for several years. Gennoinzhe is a stock strain of E. E. coli, which is currently receiving as much as 100 mg of growth hormone per 1 Liter of the culture medium. The potential for struggle is not just with dwarfism but also with short stature , but also with a weaker level of somatotropin deficiencies are discovered. Somatotropin is a key ingredient in the healing process of burns and injuries, and the hormone calcitonin (thyroid hormone) regulates the exchange of Ca 2+ in the tissues of bone. [14]

HGH or somatotropin belong to the pituitary proteins family hormones. This hormone is an estimated molecular weight of 22,000 daltons, serves within the body a crucial role as a stimulator of somatic growth.

The first time this hormone was removed and purified from the pituitary gland , which was derived from cadaveric materials. The hormone is specific to video and is the only remedy for children who suffer from its absence [22.

The effects that growth hormone has on bone development is controlled by somatomedins, insulin-like growth hormones of the polypeptide type. Somatomedins are the main source in the bloodstream are the liver and their synthesis is stimulated through growth hormone. In the control of production of somatomedins in hepatoma and other hormones like prolactin, insulin, thyroid hormones, and prolactin - are involved. Alongside in the liver, somatomedins can be synthesized in different tissues and cells particularly cartilaginous tissues, which is where they are able to act locally.

The chemical process of synthesising the hormone is complicated and costly. This is the reason somatotropin was among the first products created by genetic engineering. Genentech Inc. (USA) created an "quasi-synthetic" somatotropin gene that was constructed using a synthetic DNA fragment that encodes the 23 amino acids that make up the N-terminal component of the hormone as well as the DNA fragment that contains information about remaining somatotropin molecule. Its incorporation into a construct plasmid that contained a bacterial promoter (regulatory element that controls expression of genes) as well as the signal to initiate translation resulted in the effective transcription of the gene. This resulted in the production of growth hormone.

Somatotropins from various species, with different variations in their chemical structure, often quite significant, however they have a an obvious homology in structure. The somatotropins that have been studied in mammals and humans are made up of a single polypeptide chain that consists of 191 amino acids. They are composed of one amino acid residue, tryptophan, and four of half-cystine. The disulfide bridges (in the human somatotropin between Cys54-Cis165 and the CIS182-CIS189) create two loops in the polypeptide chain - a larger one that forms the central part that comprises the amino acid sequence as well as an additional one that is located in the C-terminal region.

The structure of somatotropins' spatial structures is defined by a high level of order. The higher proportion of non-lactic amino acids within the structure of somatotropins leads to the greater likelihood for them to form dimers as well as larger aggregates in solution.

While observing in general the evolutionary conservatism of somatotropins in various mammals, and combining it with the skepticism of its biological purpose It is important to note however that in this section, the human somatotropin is somewhat from the rest. In keeping the structure that is common to all mammals and humans, the human hormone differs in its amino acid sequence in comparison to the studied somatotropins from mammals by 34 to 35 percent. This could be the reason for the ineffectiveness of somatotropins that originate from animals in the form of growth stimulants when given to humans.

In the same way in comparing amino acid sequences from human somatotropins as well as other animals found in these proteins, it's simple to spot areas nearly identical in the structure. A high degree of evolutionary conservatism for specific parts of the chain could be a sign of their crucial functional function in delivering information on the precise purpose of the hormone.

Growth hormone, also known as"growth hormone" (STH) is made by pituitary cells with specialized functions called the somatotrophs. Somatotropic hormone is present in the pituitary of a person is approximately 5 mg, and is at least an order of magnitude more than other hormones.

Biosynthesis and secretion of the growth hormone are under complex control, including the regulation of hypothalamic factors in the first place: somatostatin inhibitory regulation and stimulating STH-releasing factor, as well as hormones-triiodothyronine and glucocorticoids, opioid peptides, etc.

The production of growth hormone is dependent on the concentration in the plasma of metabolites involved in the regulation of growth hormone that is involved in metabolism, which causes a shortage of energy substrates and also when you are asleep and in stressful conditions. [7]

The pituitary's growth hormone is extremely diverse, as a result of alternate expression of mRNA in the form of an growth hormone, as well as posttranslational modifications such as proteolysis glycosylation, phosphorylation, dimerization and the oligomerization. In response to hormone stimulation, all of these forms are expelled by the pituitary gland. within 30 minutes, they are circulated in the blood. over 50% growth hormone is present in blood plasma is in the monomeric form and 27% in a dimer, and more than 20% in an Oligomer.

In the monomeric form of the dominant growth hormone in 22kdalton STG (83 percent) and in lesser quantities twenty kdalton of STG (11%)) and approximately 6 percent are Acid forms of the hormone. The body's response to the the action of the total somatotropin of various proteins with different biological, physicochemical, and immunological characteristics .

Despite the rapid progress made in the research of growth hormones in animals and humans the mechanism by which they work at the molecular scale has not been investigated. Insufficient data regarding the spatial structure of the hormones in this group make it challenging to understand their interactions with receptors. This hinders an opportunity to study the structure-functional relation of various parts that make up the polypeptide chain. This which hinders the full utilization of the advances in protein engineering to develop analogues of growth hormones.

Recombinant growth hormone, also known as somatrem, was the second biosynthetic drug. STG is biologically pure and unaffected by contamination by viruses, was first discovered in the year 1980 by Genentech>>. Hormone produced by the genetically modified E. bacteria cells differs from hormone isolated from the pituitary additional methionine residue located at the NH 2 - end of the protein.

In the beginning, we duplicated double-stranded DNA copy of the mRNA. Then, cleavage was performed using restriction endonucleases sequence that encodes the complete amino acid structure of hormone aside from the initial 23 amino acids. Then, synthetic polypeptide was cloned that corresponds to amino acids ranging from 1 minute up to. After that, two fragments of the clone were merged, and then "tweaked" to form a two promoters (promoter - a particular DNA sequence that is essential to initiate transcription of the RNA polymerase) as well as the ribosome binding sites. The result was 2.4 mg of hormone for 1 milliliter of E.cjli culture E.cjli (100,000 hormone molecules in a cell). Growth hormone is synthesized by bacteria with an ideal MM and isn't related to any of the bacterial proteins from which it was required to separate.

Modifying the amino acid sequences of the growth hormone by altering its encoding gene is possible. synthesized as hormone analogs in bacteria. It is crucial to research the locations of the molecule's active sites and the causes of dwarfism in the molecular realm.

With the help of recombinant DNA allows you to produce growth factors and differentiation tissues by first selecting their mRNAand finding the genes they correspond to. This is applicable to somatomedin, which stimulates sulfur retention in cartilage, that occurs due to growth hormone. [7]

In 1982, it was designated and synthesized polypeptide that consists the amino acid residues 44 that have full biological activity, rizilating hypothalamic factors somatotropin (GH-RH). The introduction of GHRH can be used to make up for the absence in growth hormone. Primnenie of GH-RH can be used not only to treat of pituitary dwarfism as well as in certain forms of diabetes as well as to boost tissue regeneration in those who suffered burns that were severe.

The entire cycle of production comprises five distinct functional phases:

1) fermentation;

2.) The primary purification process of the protein

3.) purification of chromatographic data;

4.) production for the dose form

5) Quality analytical of the substance and dosage form somatogena.

A major feature of this process is that it can ensure that there is no pyrogen during the process of purification by chromatography of the protein.

An essential part of any process cycle is the an industrial complex set of quality analyses. The base of the quantity and analysis range is in accordance with WHO guidelines.

Presently, a more sophisticated drug STGch is being developed by GTC is free of aggregated forms as well as preservative Ausomatin. When it was made into single-molecule preparations STGch (e.g. ausomatina) produced large amounts of somatotropin aggregates as wastes. A novel method of changing a dimer that is not covalently linked into polymer and monomer. In addition, during this process poluchaetsyakovalentno linked dimer and polymer STGch - little studied components.

A fascinating development is the possibility of obtaining 20K version of STGch. The goal is to collect and research not just the different types of the growth hormone but additionally the immobilized growth hormone in order to create long-acting hormone. The method was developed as an original approach to making an immobilized STGch with a long-lasting effects [44.

Parallel to this, the complex technique for producing anterior pituitary hormones was designed to produce STGch comprising all species-specific, as well as specific modifications to the GTC. The key goal of the program is developing the medical product STG (somatogena) that is produced through genetic engineering.

The clinical experience has proven that, by enhancing the management of the short stature it is recommended to include a identical array of pharmaceutical preparations obtainable using various techniques or methods (MF ausomatin Somatogen). A prolonged therapy (years) STGch one drug within the body can cause decreased sensitivity. It is possible that this is due to the formation of antibodies but the principal reason is that it is important to study the receptors and the processing hormone.

Working with GTC and GTC, as well as extensive research on secrete hormones and their diverse forms, gives the chance to understand the how the system works and gain a better understanding of the mechanisms behind them. The existence of a variety of native forms of STGch body attests to their efficacy and potential use for instance when in the clinic.

When developing new drugs, STGch should first concentrate on naturally occurring forms of hormone native to us and, when appropriate to increase their size using genetic engineering. This can be done with the monomer STGch.

For the preparation of the preparations STGch GTC has successfully applied the technology needed to make various industrial and other hormones from the adenohypophysis (LGch, FSGch, TTGch and others.). It is important to optimize production by introducing modern methods (affinity chromatography, etc.) Superpurity's are receiving hormones to support advanced technology. It is important to expand the use and production of sets of immunomikroanaliza anterior pituitary hormones to aid in biotechnology and diagnostics. to control your production of antibodies at various scales that are standardized, for the development of new drugs STGch that include immobilized. [2]

The fact that the growth hormone influences minerals, protein, fat metabolism, and acts on the cell level and not the organs of target and is anabolic offers good chances of its use for stimulating of healing processes and the treatment of various illnesses. A more thorough study of these issues is required, along with potential use of different variants and modified forms STGch, which is a present and future issues.

In Biotechnology, insulin is prepared.

Insulin is a peptide hormone that is found in the pancreatic islets in Langerhans is the principal treatment for the condition diabetes. The cause of this disease is an insulin deficiency and is characterized by elevated amounts of glucose present in blood. In the past, insulin was came from bovine pancreas and porcines. It is distinct in comparison to human insulin 3 amino acid substitutes and poses an increased risk for allergic reactions specifically for children. The widespread use of insulin for therapeutic purposes is limited by the high price and the lack of resources. The chemical modification of animal insulin, the product is to be indistinguishable from human insulin, however, it also means an increase in appreciation for the product.

EliLilly company has been in operation since 1982. It has been producing genetically engineered insulins on the basis of separate synthesis from E. colie A- and B-chains. Cost of production is reduced significantly. the insulin produced is similar to human. In 1980 in the media there have been reports of the cloning of the proinsulin gene as a precursor to hormones, that is rolling in the maturing form of restricted proteolysis.

To treat diabetes, there's also to encapsulation technology pancreatic cells inside capsules after introduction to the body of the patient, will produce insulin within one year.

Company Integrated Genetics launched a Folly kulostimuliruyuschego and luteinizing hormone. The peptides comprise two subunits. The issue on the table is of industrial synthesis of oligopeptides in the nervous system enkephalins comprised of 5 amino acid residues and endorphins which are analogues of morphine. To make them useful, these peptides to relieve pain, promote a positive mood, improve efficiency, focus and improves memory, clean sleeping and awakefulness. A good example of the successful use of genetic engineering techniques could be the synthesis of p-endorphins from hybrid proteins based on the technique previously described for the other hormone somatostatin.

Methods to get human insulin

In the past, the primary method for producing insulin for therapeutic use was the separation of hormone analogs from the natural sources (pancreatic islets of cattle and pigs). In the 20th century of the century, researchers discovered that the insulins of porcine and bovine (which are most like human insulin with respect to the amino acid structure as well as in) within the human body show similar activity to human insulin. Then, it took a long duration of treatment for those suffering from type I with the insulin of swine or bovine. However, after a while, it was observed that some humans, it is possible to build antibodies against porcine and bovine insulin, and thus reducing their effects.

However the benefit for this approach is its availability insulin-producing fuelstock (bovine and porcine insulins can be easily obtained in huge quantities) and has played an important role in the creation of the initial method of making human insulin. This technique is known as semi-synthetic.

This method of making human insulin, which is a raw porcine insulin, it is made available. The purified porcine insulin, the C-terminal B-chain octapeptide was synthesized, and after that, the C-terminal C-terminal Octapeptide human insulin. It was then chemically linked to the insulin, then deprotected and finally purified made. The insulin preparations obtained show 100% identity to the human insulin hormone. The biggest drawback with this technique is cost of the insulin that is produced (even the synthesis of octapeptide chemicals is costly, especially on the industrial setting).

Human insulin is generally , can be obtained via two different methods that are: modification of an enzyme that is synthesized from porcine blood, and genetic engineering.

In the first scenario the procedure is founded on the fact that insulin from porcine is different from insulin in humans in that it replaces an insulin at the end of C the B chain called Ala30Thr. The substitution of threonine for alanine occurs through enzyme-catalyzed decleavage and joining -alanine in place of the protected carboxyl Threonine is that is present in the reaction mix in an excessive amount. After the cleavage of the protective O-t-butyl-group, human insulin.

The insulin protein was first created for commercial use made using the recombinant DNA technique. There are two primary methods for the genetically modified human insulin. In the first, the separation is accomplished (various producer strains) creation of two strands and then an unfolding of the molecules (the development of disulfide-bridges) and the dissociation of isoforms. In the second, you will obtain the precursor (proinsulin) then an enzymatic digestion using trypsin and carboxypeptidase B , to create an active hormone. It is currently the most preferred method to supply insulin as a precursor, thereby ensuring the proper closure of bridges of disulfide (in the event that separate chains of receiving that have by successive cycles of denaturation the renaturation process and the isoform segregation). [9]

Both approaches can be an separate preparations of the starting components (AB-chains as well as proinsulin) and also as part of the fusion proteins. Alongside the B- and A-chains as well as proinsulin, fusion proteins the composition could be:

1.) Protein carriers allows the transport for the protein fusion into the periplasmic region of the cell or medium for culture

2.) affinity component that is significantly aids in the isolation of the Fusion protein.

These two components could be present simultaneously inside the hybrid proteins. Furthermore, when creating hybrid proteins, using the multimeric principles (i.e. in the fusion protein there are multiple copies of the polypeptide you want) will significantly increase the yield. [10]

Proinsulin expression Proinsulin expression E. coli cells ..

We chose the strain JM 109 N1864 that was incorporated into a plasmid nucleotide sequence that expresses an fusion protein which is composed of a linear proinsulin linked to the methionine methionine residue at its N-terminal until the final component of Staphylococcus aureus. Growing the recombinant strain in filled with biomass cells produces the fusion protein that starts isolation, production and subsequent transformation within the tube that results in insulin. Another group obtained, in the form of a bacterial expression system an recombinant fusion protein made up of human proinsulin. It is connected to methionine through a the polyhistidine "tail." It was isolated by column chromatography that chelates Ni-agarose in inclusion bodies, and digested with cyanogen oxybromide. The researchers found that the protein that was isolated is an S-sulphonated. Mass spectrometric and mapping analysis of the proinsulin, purified using Ion Exchange Chromatography on the anion exchanger as well as an RP (reverse Phase) HPLC (high performance liquid chromatography) revealed evidence of bridges between disulfide as well as similar disulfide bridges to those of proinsulin native to human. The paper also discussed the development of a novel and improved methods of making human insulin through genetic engineering of prokaryotic cells. The researchers found that the insulin resulting from the process has shape and biological function is the same as hormone extracted from pancreas. [13]

In recent times, more attention has been paid to the streamlined process for creating recombinant insulin through genetic engineering. This resulted in a fusion protein composed of the leader peptide from interleukin that is attached to the tip of the N-proinsulin through an lysine residue. Protein is effectively expressed and localized within inclusion bodies. After the isolation of the protein was then cleaved using trypsin to extract an insulin-like peptide and the C-peptide. A different group of researchers performed in a similar way. A fusion protein that consists of two proinsulins that are synthetic and staphylococcal binding protein A domains IgG that is located within inclusion bodies, however is more active in expression. Protein is isolated through affinity chromatography with IgG and is then treated by carboxypeptidase B and trypsin. The insulin and C-peptide that resulted was purified using RP HPLC. In the process of creating a fusion structure, there is a significant mass ratio of the protein carrier as well as the polypeptide of choice. In this case, the creation of fusion structures, in which the carrier polypeptide was made using protein that binds to human serum albumin. To it were attached one, three, and seven C-peptides. C-peptides were joined with the "head-tail" together with amino acid spacers that carry the restriction website Sfi I and two arginine residues at the start as well as at the conclusion of the spacer for the next digesting of trypsin in the proteins. HPLC product for cleavage demonstrated that the C-peptide cleavage process takes place in a quantitative manner, allowing to employ a technique of multimeric synthetic genes that produce the desired polypeptide at commercial scale.

Proinsulin mutant was prepared that contained a replacement for Arg32Tyr. In combination, cleavage and fusion of the protein by carboxypeptidase B and trypsin, it produced native insulin as well as a C-peptide with a tyrosine atom. After labeling using 125I, it's widely utilized in radioimmunoassays. [14]

Elimination of the insulin.

Insulin is used to be used in the production of medicines and other pharmaceuticals, is designed to be of the highest purity. Thus, a high-performance check for the pureness of products produced at each step of the production. Previously the RP and RI (ion exchange), HPLC were characterized proinsulin-S-sulfonate, proinsulin, separate A- and B-chains and their S-sulfonates. Additionally, particular focus is paid to fluorescent insulin derivatives [1414. In this paper, the authors assessed the usefulness and useful chromatographic techniques in studying the human insulin production and performed regulation chromatographic processes to effectively distinguish and characterize the end products. The authors separated the products using bifunctional variations from insulin-sorbents (hydrophobic RP HPLC and ion exchange) and also demonstrated the possibility of regulating separation selectivity by varying the contribution of each interaction and achieving

167

higher effectiveness for the isolation of similar to the proteins' analogs. Additionally, strategies are being developed for automating and acceleration techniques to measure the purity and amount of insulin. Research has been reported on the possibility of making use of RP HPLC using electrochemical detection to determine the amount of insulin, and the method for determining insulin islets isolated from Langerhans through immunoaffinity chromatography using spectrometry. The research explored the possibility of quick mikroopredeleniya in the form of capillary electrophores with detection of lasers. Analyzing is done using the addition of the known amounts of insulin labeled by the phenyl isothiocyanate (FITC) as well as it is the Fab Monoclonal Antibodies fragment that react to insulin. Both insulins labeled and traditional react with the Fab share. The insulin labeled with FITC is complex reaction with Fab shares for thirty seconds. [12]

Recently, there have been an abundance of studies have been dedicated to improving techniques for making insulin as well as the development of formulas made from it. For example, U.S. patented gepatospetsificheskie insulin analogs are structurally different from the natural hormone by introducing into the position 13 - 15 and 19 of the A-chain and position 16 of the B chain of other amino acid residues. The resulting analogs are utilized in a range of parenteral (intravenous intramuscular, subcutaneous,) and nasal dosage forms, in capsules with special properties for the treatment of diabetes. Particularly important is the development of dosage forms that do not require injection. The first reported on the development of the macromolecular system for oral administration of insulin is immobilized in the context of water-based polymer modified inhibitors for proteolytic enzymes. The effectiveness of this formulation is between 70 and 80% of the effectiveness of the native insulin that is that is administered subcutaneously. In a different study the drug was made by with a single-stage incubation of insulin with erythrocytes in the ratio of 1-4 100, with the addition of an agent for coupling. The authors discuss the creation of a drug that has an activity of 1,000 units. • G. Maintaining its all-encompassing activity when administered orally and stored for a period of decades in an lyophilized format.

In addition , they are developing new dosage forms and drugs that are based on insulin, they are also working on new methods to solve the issue of diabetes. This is why the cDNA was transfected with glucose transporter GLUT2 protein that was previously stable transfected with full length of cDNA insulin HEP G2 in cells. The resultant clone HEP Insgl increases glucose levels close to the normal insulin secretion process and increases the response of the secretory system to the release of other stimulants. When using immunoelectron microscopes in cells, they found that insulin-containing granules appear morphologically like the b-cell granules found in Langerhans islets. In the present, scientists have seriously considered whether it is possible to use treating type-1 diabetes "artificial B-cells" generated through genetic engineering. [12]

In addition to solving real-world issues, the mechanisms of the action of insulin and insulin's mechanisms of action, as well as structures-function relationships of the protein. One method is to conduct an analysis of the various insulin derivatives, and analyzing their physicochemical and immunological characteristics. As previously mentioned, there are there are a variety of insulin production strategies are that are based on the reception from the hormone as precursor (proinsulin) and then an enzyme-mediated digestion of insulin, and C-peptide. As of now, C-peptide exhibits biological activity, and it could be utilized for therapeutic purposes alongside insulin. The next installment in this series will focus on the biological and physicochemical characteristics of C-peptide as well as methods of its production.

Biotechnology's role in industrial production of non-peptide hormonal compounds specifically steroids. Techniques for microbiological transformations permit to dramatically decrease the number of chemical synthesis processes that produce cortisone is an adrenal hormone utilized to treat Rheumatoid Arthritis. In the process of producing steroids are commonly employed immobilized microbial cells e.g. Arthrobacterglobiformis, for the synthesis of hydrocortisone prednisolone. There are advancements in the preparation of the thyroid hormone thyroxine by microalgae. [14]

4. Preparation of interferons, interleukinsand interferons blood factors

Interferons are injected into both animal and human cells as a result of virus infection. They are antiviral. The mechanism behind the action of interferons isn't completely comprehended. It is believed in particular that interferons hinder the penetration of virus particles into cells. Interferons boost the function in the immune system and stop the growth of cancerous cells. Every aspect of the actions of interferons are vital for their therapeutic application.

Interferons are the main ingredient in interferons.

Differentiate between a-, band g and e'interferon, produced by leukocytes, fibroblasts of connective tissue epithelial cells and T-lymphocytes. The most significant are the three first categories. Interferons comprise amino acid residues ranging from 146 to 166 as well as b - and g-interferon linked to sugar residues (glycosylated). Prior to the advent methods of engineering genetics,, interferons were obtained from blood donors up to 1 g of interferon crude from one milliliter of blood, which is around one dose for the injection...

Methods for preparation of interferon from human cells human blood leukocytes stimulated by viruses or other inducers.

The biggest drawback with the methods used to produce interferons is that they are contaminated by human viruses. possibility of contamination in the end product, like the hepatitis B as well as C virus, the immunodeficiency virus and many others.

The current research suggests a efficient method to produce interferon microbiological synthesis , which allows getting the desired product at an extremely high yield using relatively cheap beginning materials. The method used allows for the creation of optimal the expression of bacterial the structural genes and regulatory elements that regulate the expression of that gene.

As microorganisms that can be used as starting points, they use various types of designs Pichia pastoris varieties, Pseudomonas putida and Escherichia bacteria.

The drawback of the use of P. pastoris for interferon producer is that it is very difficult to make. conditions for fermentation in this type of yeast. They must ensure the amount of inducer, specifically Methanol, throughout the process of biosynthesis.

The main drawback to the use of strains of Ps. putida fermentation is the complexity at a lower amount in expression (10 mg interferon in 1 Liter of the culture medium). It is more efficient to use Escherichia-coli strains.

Many plasmids, and variant strains of E. coli, expressing interferon. These include strains belonging to E. coli ATCC 31633 and 31644 containing plasmid Z-pBR322 (Psti) Z-pBR 322 (Pstl) or HclN SN 35 -AHL6 (SU 1764515) is a variant of E. coli pINF- (SU 1312961), a strain of (SU 1312961) is a variant that is part of E. coli pINF- F-Pa (AU 1,312,962) is a variant that belongs to E.Coli SG 20050 with plasmid P280/21FN (Kravchenko VV and al. Bioorganic Chemistry, 1987, t.13, no. 9. s.1186-1193), E.Coli SG 20050 strain carrying the plasmid PINF14 (SU 1703691), E.coli SG 20050 strain carrying the plasmid called PINF16 (RU 2054041) and a. The disadvantage of the technologies built on the use of this strain is its incompatibility and the lack of expression levels in the nterferona.

Alongside the features of the strains utilized, the selection of strains is largely dependent on the efficacy of the technology used to isolate and purify interferon.

A method for creating interferon that involves cultivating cells of Ps. putida destruction biomass treatment with polyethyleneimine and fractionation using ammonium sulfate hydrophobic chromatography fenilsilohrome C 80 pH fractionation lysate diafiltration and its concentration Ion exchange chromatography on DE-52 cellulose, which elutes using the pH gradient and ion exchange chromatography, which results in the eluent cellulose-CM-52, its concentration via an emulsion filter and the gel filtration process on Sephadex G-100 (SU 1640996). The drawback of this method in addition to a complex multiple-stage fermentation, is the preparation for the product to be produced.

Also , the method of producing interferon that involves cultivating an E. coli strain, E.coli the SG 20050/pIF16 in LB-broth in shaker flask that is thermostatically controlled, then centrifugation, biomass washing buffer, and Sonication to break up the cells. The resulting lysate is then centrifuged and washed using a 3M urea in the buffer, then dissolved in an guanidine-chloride solution in the buffer, sonicated, conducted oxidative sulfitoliz dialysis in the presence of the 8M urea solution, and renaturation, and final two-stage chromatography of the CM-52 cellulose, and Sephadex G-50 (RU 2054041).

The main drawback to this technique is its ineffective steps in the isolation and purification. Particularly, it is related to using ultrasonic treatment for the products and then dialyzed oxidatively which results in unstable interferon release and inability to utilize this method to produce industrial quantities of interferon.

The most similar analog (prototype) could be described as an approach to produce human leukocyte interferon by cultivating the recombinant strain of E.coli and the resultant biomass being frozen at temperatures that is not more than -70 degrees C and then thawing. This causes the destruction of microorganisms using lysozyme to remove DNA and RNA by incubating DNA-ase lysate and then removal of the chosen insoluble form of interferon by washing the buffer solution containing detergent, dissolving interferon precipitate within guanidine hydrochloride solution and a single-stage renaturation and of ynoy by Ion Exchange chromatography. It is the same E.coli SS5 producing strain obtained by recombination with pSS5 that contains three promoters: Plac Pt7, Ptrp and an alpha-interferon molecule with introduction of nucleotide substitutions.

Expression of the interferon strain of E.coli SS5, containing this plasmid, is controlled by 3 promoters: Pt7 Pt7, and Ptrp. Interferon levels are around 800 mg per liter of suspension cell. [eleven]

The disadvantage of the technique is the inability to process enzyme-mediated cell destruction as well as the DNA and the RNA of the microorganism and chromatographic purification in one step of interferon. This can cause instability in the interferon isolating process, which results in lower quality and restricts the possibilities of using the above method to manufacture industrially produced interferon.

The drawbacks of this plasmid strains resulting from its use , are not controlled by the strong promoter of plasmid T7 in the strain E. coli BL21 (DE3) that has the T7 RNA polymerase gene is located under the lac operon promoter is continuously "flows". In the cell, the synthesis of interferon continues to occur and leads to the dissociation of plasmids and decreases the viability of cells in the strain and, consequently, reduced yield of interferon.

In order to produce large quantities of interferon, use monolayer embryonic chick cells or humans with white blood cells that have been infected by a particular kind of virus. To collect IFN create a specific virus-cell systems.

Human cells were able to isolate the gene responsible for production of IFN. Human exogenous IFN is produced by the recombinant DNA technique. IFN-s is a cDNA isolation process. in the following manner:

1.) Human leukocytes are isolated mRNA is separated in accordance with its size. perform reverse transcription, and is then inserted into the location that is modified by the plasmid.

2.) The result of the transformation is E. E. coli. The results are divided into groups which are distinguished.

3.) Each clone group were hybridized with IFN - MRNA.

4.) The resulting hybrids that contain cDNA and hRNK the isolated mRNA is processed by its broadcast protein synthesis process [4].

5.) Examine the antiviral interferon effect of each mix, the consequent broadcast. Group that has demonstrated interferon activities have a cDNA-based clone that has been hybridized to IFN mRNA. Repeatly find a clone that contains the complete length IFN human CDNA.

Presently, a-, band g-interferon were produced successfully by the use in genetically engineered varieties of E. coli , yeast and invertebrate cells cultured (Drosophila) and mammal. Interferon that is genetically engineered can be isolated using monoclonal antibody. For P-interferon and y, it is recommended to utilize prokaryotic makers since prokaryotes are not glycosylated proteins. Some companies, for instance Bioferon (Germany) do not employ genetically engineered mutants and fibroblasts that have been cultured in vitro.

Interferons are utilized to treat illnesses caused by herpesviruses or rabies, such as hepatitis Tsitomegalo virus that can lead to dangerous heart failure and for protection against viral diseases. Interferons inhalation from aerosols can stop the formation of acute respiratory diseases. One of the most interesting aspects is that interferons specifically a-interferons in particular, may cause symptoms of catarrhal (runny nose and fever.). The risk of adverse side effects is particularly severe during the long-term therapeutic use of interferons needed for the treatment of cancer. [13]

Interferons can have a therapeutic impact on patients suffering from breast cancer as well as skin, throat and lungs, as well as brain diffuse myeloma and Sarcoma. These two illnesses are common among people with Acquired Immune Deficiency. Interferons also aid for treating MS.

Genetic engineering techniques allow the modification of interferons to be modified. Interferons' antiviral properties vary depending on amino acid substitutes (J. Werenne, 1983). The US company makes CetusCorporation b-interferon which is an amino acid series that cysteine in position 17 has been substituted to the sequence. This enhances the therapeutic efficacy of the drug since it blocks it from creating the inactive dimer in the in vitro environment b -inter-

Feron through disulfide bonds formed between cysteine residues at position 17. The most promising possibility is modification through the creation of Interferon-Hybrid compounds (E. D. Sverdlov 1984).

Getting interleukins

Interleukins are comparatively small (approximately 150 amino acids) polypeptides that participate within the immuno-response. Interleukin-1 is a class of blood leukocytes, namely macrophages. In response to the antigen , triggers the proliferation (proliferation) of the T-helper cell (a subset of T-lymphocytes) which produce interleukin-2. This triggers the proliferation of different types of T lymphocytes: T-killer cells, T-helper cell T suppressor as well as B-lymphocytes that make antibodies. The IL-2 molecule T cells, they release regulatory proteins , lymphokines that stimulate elements that are part of our immune system. they are produced as an interleukins primary therapy for immune-related disorders. They are produced through cloning of the genes responsible for the same within E. coll lymphocytes or by invitro. English as well as Japanese celltechLtd SakyoCompany offers the interleukin-1 bacterium that is synthesized in a genetic engineering as well as another agent called tyulipeptidnym, which is a tumor necrosis -. It is used to treat a variety of neoplastic disorders [44

Interleukins, bioactive substances created by leukocytes, and play a role in interactions between cells. Interleukins are the primary contributors to the formation of an immune reaction to microorganisms and the initiation of inflammatory reactions of antitumor immunity , and so on. Cytokines, referred to as interleukins, and ranging from 1-25 are not an exclusive subset of cytokines and are referred to as "interleukins" that have been used historically. Interleukins can be classified into growth factors, cytokines that promote inflammation and lymphocyte differentiation, the chemokines and cytokines with individual regulatory properties. In the production of interleukin Russia has made significant progress. The creation of two recombinant medicines: Roncoleukin and Betaleukin.

Conclusion

Presently, there is no doubt that the future of the pharmaceutical industry will is largely controlled by biotechnology. In contrast to traditional medications, chemical synthesis techniques, they are utilized in the field of pharmaceutical biotechnology which allows the creation of compounds that are the foundation of pharmaceuticals (primarily proteins) which are often identical to natural. The major benefit of the drugs made by biotechnology is their high specificity regards to the elements related to the development and emergence of diseases. This technique has enabled the development of various medications to treat diseases such as cardiovascular diseases, cancer as well as neurodegenerative diseases.

Prior to the introduction in recombinant technology several drugs based upon human proteins were available in very small quantities and their production was extremely expensive and the mechanism behind their biological actions was unclear. Since the start of the evolution of genetic engineering, we believed that with the new technology we would be able to access the full variety of these preparations in quantities sufficient to be effective in clinical practice. This was the case. The preparations that were obtained by biotechnological have been approved for use in a wide range.